Graphic Design of Scheld'Apen

Selected and designed by Benny Van den Meulengracht-Vrancx and Bent Vande Sompele.

With texts by Pieter Willems, Roel Griffioen and Pia Jacques.

Artwork (2005 07 PB) on previous page, by Janus 'Prutpuss' Lemaire.

Legend: each work is specified by date plus type of artwork, 'F' for Flyer, 'P' for Poster, 'PB' for Program Booklet. '›' refers to work on the next page, '‹' refers to work on the previous page.

Published and produced by
Bruno Devos at Stockmans Art Books.
First edition, printed in Duffel, Belgium in 2023.
ISBN 9789464363395

Graphic Design of Scheld'Apen

A selection of works from the physical archive of collected posters, flyers and program booklets, brought together by Benny Van den Meulengracht-Vrancx and Bent Vande Sompele.

Preface
Pieter Willems

The preface by Pieter Willems is written in Dutch, because you can't translate his writings.

Ergens, verscholen in de Antwerpse Zuidrand, omzoomd door eeuwenoude kastanjeschimmels en steunend op een fundament van gedumpte nazipetrol bevond zich ooit een sanitair heiligdom voor avontuurlijke ontlasters.

Een hardnekkige urinewasem en een penetrante putlucht dansten er op het door hun duivelspact gedolven graf van ene mijnheer Proper. Desondanks weerhield deze wetenschap een uitgebreide schare aan zeikerds en schijtluizen met een scherpe blik en een talent voor vervoering er niet van zich in het illustere rioolrijk te begeven.

Sterker nog, menigeen bracht meer tijd in het olfactorisch oorlogsgebied door dan strikt noodzakelijk was. Snotneuzen en doorzetters konden zich blijven vergapen aan nonsensicale deurconversaties, de onontkoombare grafische gruwel die men tags noemt en de immer muterende murale collage van spuitbuskunst, zwart wit kopij, glossy kleurenprint, een halve flyer en zeefdruk van beperkte oplage.

Veel te kort door de bocht gescheurd zou men kunnen stellen dat dit kleinood de gedrukte versie van die beruchte toiletten van Scheld'Apen is.

Het is eruit.

Scheld'Apen.

Ooit het slechtst bewaarde geheim van de Antwerpse oproerkraaier, wereldverbeteraar, tuig van de richel, wildkampeerder en meerwaardezoeker.

Een plek die meer stichtende leden dan bezoekers telde.

Waar elke nieuwe dag logischerwijs toch niet meer hetzelfde als vroeger was.

Waar grootspraak, bescheidenheid, hoge of lage wenkbrauwen en een kwinkslag steevast op vinkenslag lagen.

In die toiletruimte werd dus omzeggens de kiem gelegd van dit opus.

De sanitaire esthetiek van Scheld'Apen fascineerde twee Apejoeng in die mate dat ze afzonderlijk van elkaar een Scheld'Apen archief aanlegden. De ene in een mooie doos met plastiekjes, de andere koos voor een kartonnen doos. Dat ze onder, in of naast de vleugels van Scheld'Apen concerteerden, organiseerden, labels oprichtten, exposeerden, de WC (!) van een make-over voorzagen, op werkkamp gingen, Scheld'Apen een zomer lang overnamen... laten we dan nog onvermeld.

Ondertussen bleef het huis al dan niet geautoriseerd drukwerk braken.

Helaas, zoals een Waaslands scribent het ooit neerschreef: "Alles moet weg".

Scheld'Apen ruimde plaats voor een Antwerpse voetbaltempel die nooit gebouwd zou worden en verhuisde naar de binnenstad om daar met Het Bos een nieuwe werking uit de grond te stampen die toch niet meer hetzelfde als vroeger is.

Het officiële archief werd na een wijdverspreide oproep nog uitgebreid – die twee frisse neuzen waren lang niet de enigen met een S'A archief in eigen beheer – waarop het verhuisklaar werd gemaakt.

Beeldfabriek Afreux worstelde zich er al eens door, maar wegens tijds- en geldgebrek stierf die eerste poging een stille dood en verdween alles terug in kartonnen dozen.

Godzijdank, zoals een Mechels tv-maker het ooit stelde: "Alles komt terug".

Zo ook dat vermaledijde archief.

Het Apejoeng van weleer verloor enkele plukken wilde haren en mat zichzelf zowaar een zekere sérieux aan.

Toen beeldend kunstenaar Benny Van den Meulgracht-Vrancx en muzikant en vormgever Bent Vande Sompele in alle ernst aan Het Bos voorstelden iets met dat archief te doen, vond er een uniek geval van snelle besluitvorming plaats aan de Ankerrui.

Vergaderingen werden belegd, residenties vastgelegd en een lange, doch plezierige obstakelbaan afgelegd. Gedurende drie residentieperiodes nestelden BentenBenny zich in Het Bos en werd al het voorradige fysieke beeldmateriaal verzameld en gedigitaliseerd. Van goed ingelichte bronnen vernamen we dat er ook buiten die perioden stiekem archivaris werd gespeeld, waarvoor hulde.

Organisatoren, bezoekers, fans, leden en spreekwoordelijk meubilair werden uitgenodigd en ondervraagd, evenementen werden opgelijst en als ware rechercheurs baanden ze zich een weg door een rijk verleden.

De hele operatie vond plaats onder de auspiciën van drie wijzen die Nico Dockx, Tile Vos en David Van der Weken in het diepst van hun hart zijn.

Hulde.

Bruno Devos van Stockmans Art Books toonde zich dan weer bereid om dit geval uit te geven.

Weerom, hulde!

Wat hierna volgt is geen chronologisch overzicht of inventaris van tien ton Scheld'Apengrafiek. Geen historiek, wel een historisch hebbeding. Dit boek omvat een weloverwogen selectie van meer dan 250 beelden die het levenslicht zagen binnen het tijdsbestek 1998-2013 en waarmee de samenstellers met een artistieke focus composities, dan wel juxtaposities creëerden die de diversiteit aan beelden, stijlen, technieken en dragers van Scheld'Apens communicatie benadrukken.

Bent Vande Sompele en Benny Van den Meulengracht-Vrancx vertellen een beeldverhaal dat voor zich spreekt, maar niet pretendeert de waarheid te vertellen.

Wij wensen u veel kijk- en bladergenot.

Uw Scheld'Apen

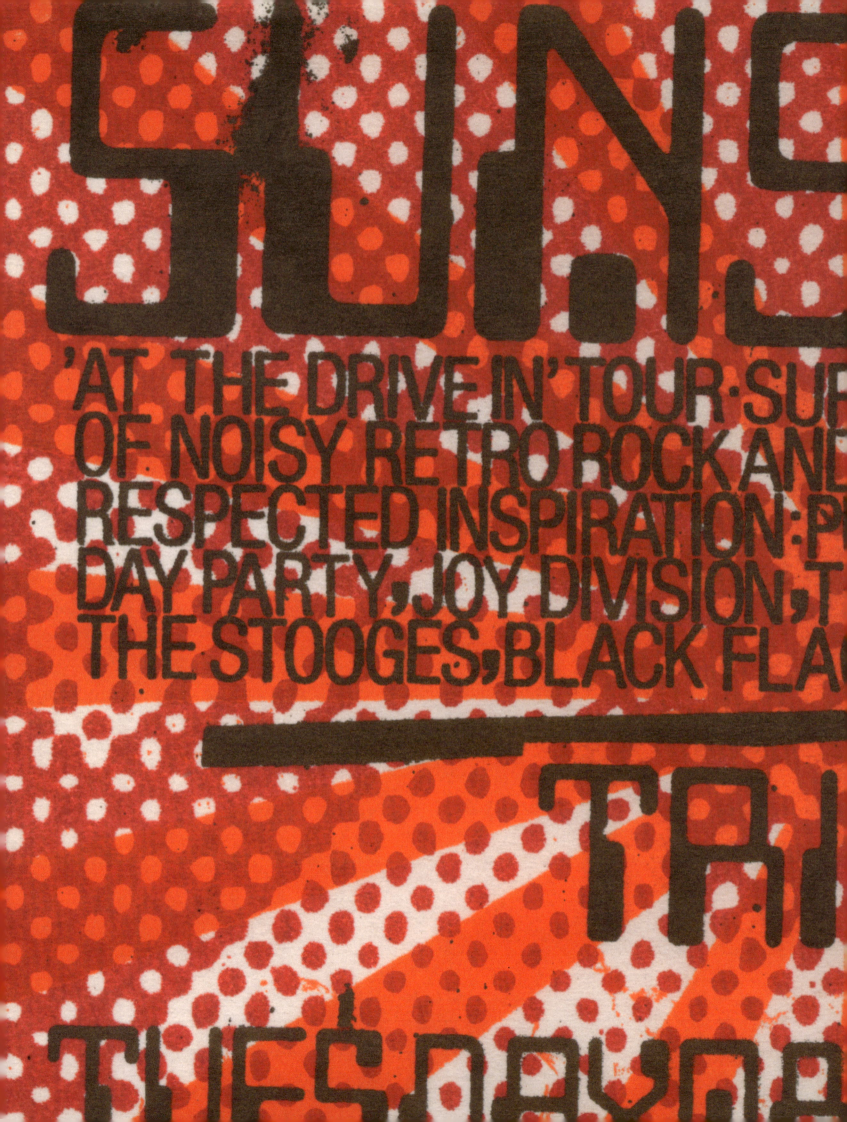

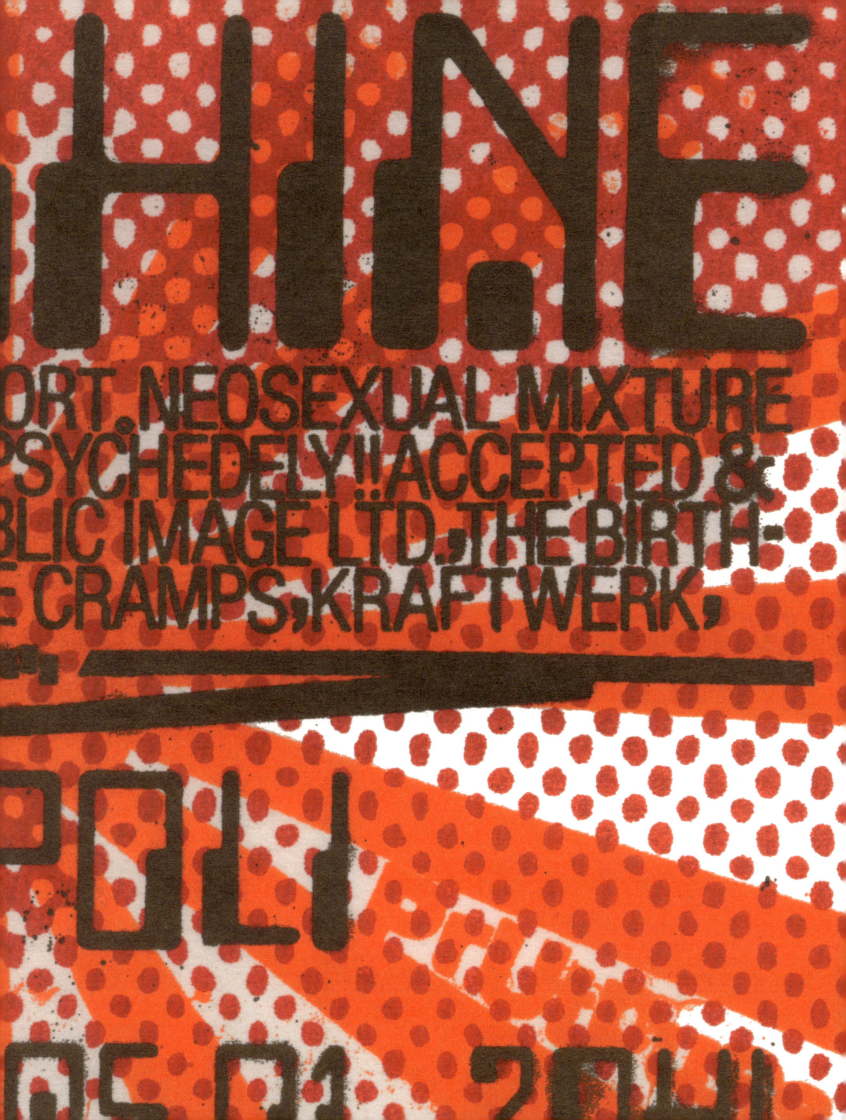

3
POUPI WHOOPY
RELEASE PARTY

14 | 02 | 09 | 21H

VALENTIJN'S RELEASE PARTY VAN
POUPI WHOOPY 3

ACTS
DIEVEN ACT by MURIELLE EN JEN
HAREM DEVILLES in a
BARBARA ROM show
CREAMY CARO

LUXE VOXE
KLEKE

DO. 1 FEB.

AT THE SCHELDA'PEN
D'HERBOUVILLEKAAI 36
VANAF 20.00 U

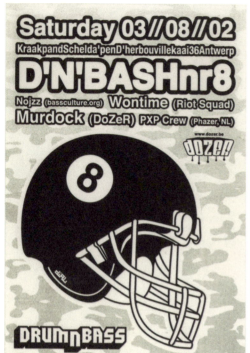
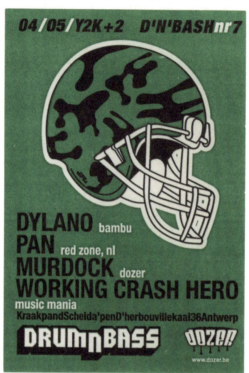

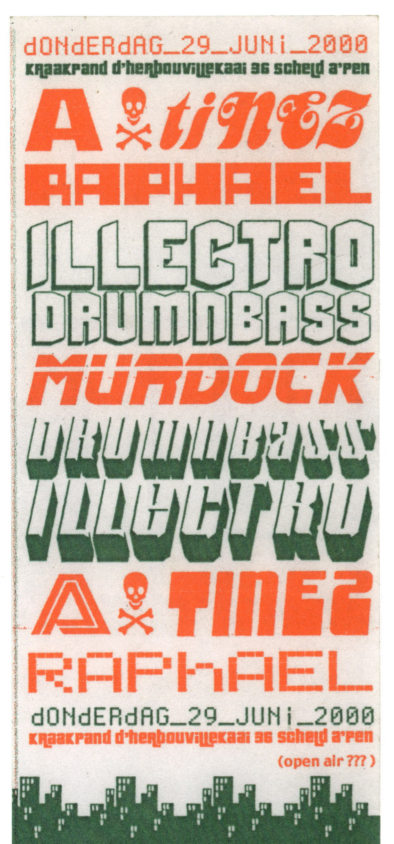
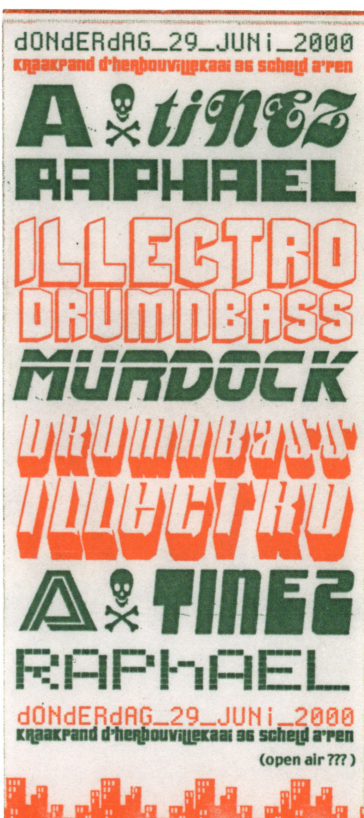

24032001

DOZER

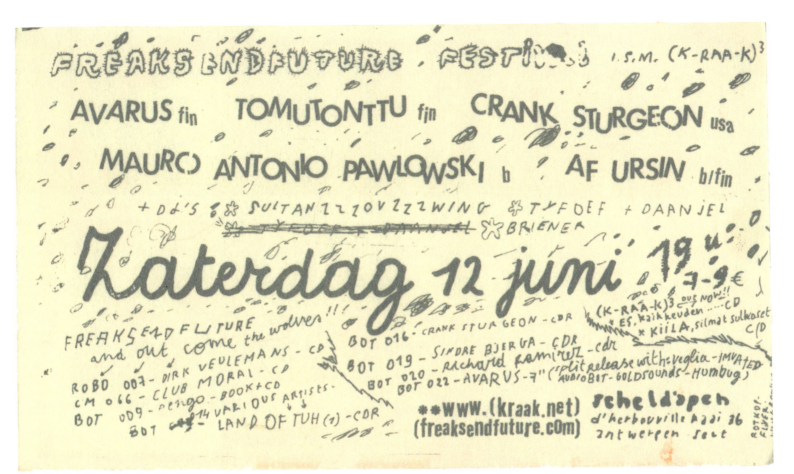

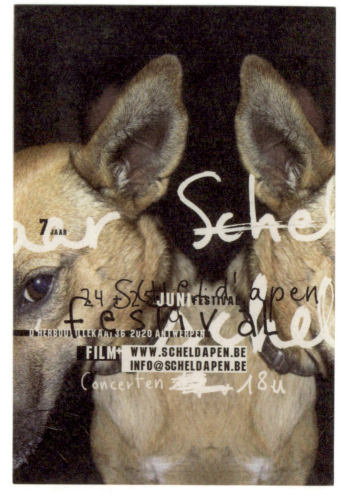

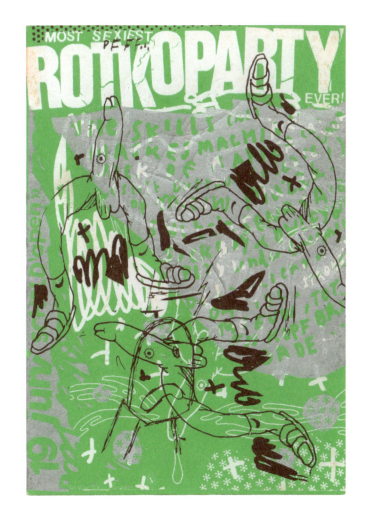

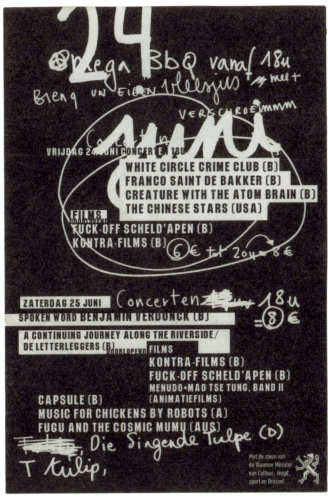

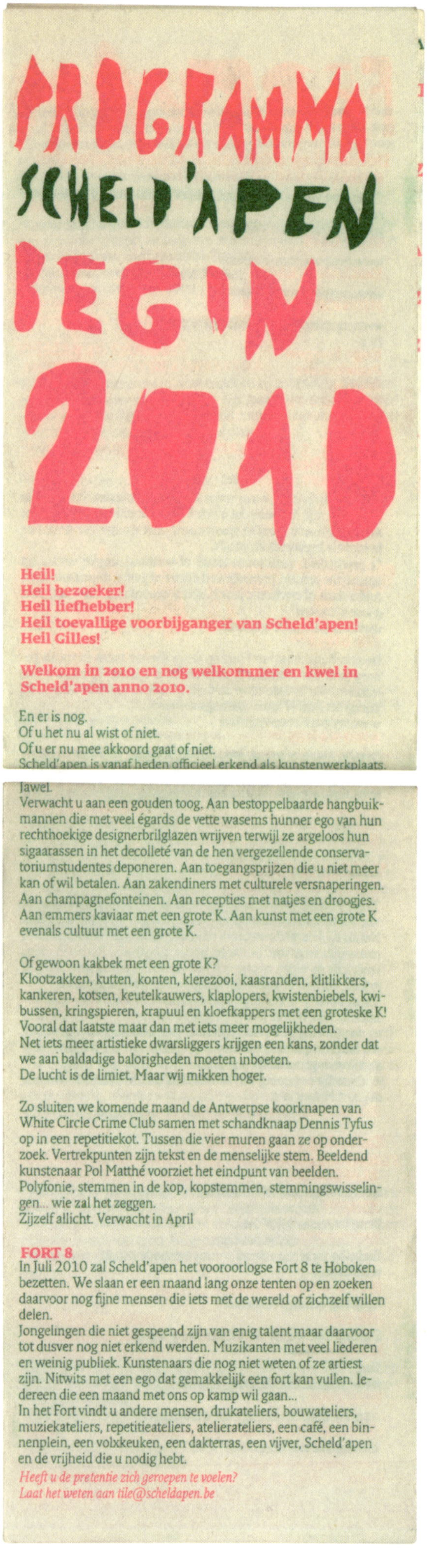

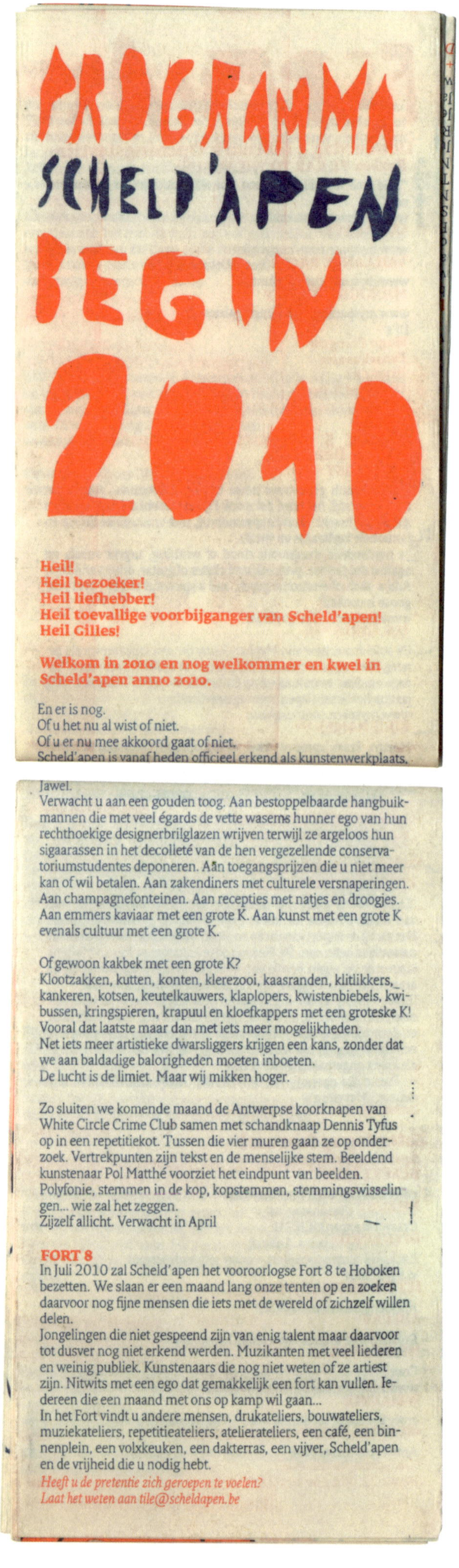

PROGRAMMA SCHELD'APEN BEGIN 2010

Heil!
Heil bezoeker!
Heil liefhebber!
Heil toevallige voorbijganger van Scheld'apen!
Heil Gilles!

Welkom in 2010 en nog welkommer en kwel in Scheld'apen anno 2010.

En er is nog.
Of u het nu al wist of niet.
Of u er nu mee akkoord gaat of niet.
Scheld'apen is vanaf heden officieel erkend als kunstenwerkplaats.
Jawel.
Verwacht u aan een gouden toog. Aan bestoppelbaarde hangbuikmannen die met veel égards de vette wasems hunner ego van hun rechthoekige designerbrilglazen wrijven terwijl ze argeloos hun sigaarassen in het decolleté van de hen vergezellende conservatoriumstudentes deponeren. Aan toegangsprijzen die u niet meer kan of wil betalen. Aan zakendiners met culturele versnaperingen. Aan champagnefonteinen. Aan recepties met natjes en droogjes. Aan emmers kaviaar met een grote K. Aan kunst met een grote K evenals cultuur met een grote K.

Of gewoon kakbek met een grote K?
Klootzakken, kutten, konten, klerezooi, kaasranden, klitlikkers, kankeren, kotsen, keutelkauwers, klaplopers, kwistenbiebels, kwibussen, kringspieren, krapuul en kloefkappers met een groteske K!
Vooral dat laatste maar dan met iets meer mogelijkheden.
Net iets meer artistieke dwarsliggers krijgen een kans, zonder dat we aan baldadige balorigheden moeten inboeten.
De lucht is de limiet. Maar wij mikken hoger.

Zo sluiten we komende maand de Antwerpse koorknapen van White Circle Crime Club samen met schandknaap Dennis Tyfus op in een repetitiekot. Tussen die vier muren gaan ze op onderzoek. Vertrekpunten zijn tekst en de menselijke stem. Beeldend kunstenaar Pol Matthé voorziet het eindpunt van beelden.
Polyfonie, stemmen in de kop, kopstemmen, stemmingswisselingen... wie zal het zeggen.
Zijzelf allicht. Verwacht in April

FORT 8
In Juli 2010 zal Scheld'apen het vooroorlogse Fort 8 te Hoboken bezetten. We slaan er een maand lang onze tenten op en zoeken daarvoor nog fijne mensen die iets met de wereld of zichzelf willen delen.
Jongelingen die niet gespeend zijn van enig talent maar daarvoor tot dusver nog niet erkend werden. Muzikanten met veel liederen en weinig publiek. Kunstenaars die nog niet weten of ze artiest zijn. Nitwits met een ego dat gemakkelijk een fort kan vullen. Iedereen die een maand met ons op kamp wil gaan...
In het Fort vindt u andere mensen, drukateliers, bouwateliers, muziekateliers, repetitieateliers, atelierateliers, een café, een binnenplein, een volxkeuken, een dakterras, een vijver, Scheld'apen en de vrijheid die u nodig hebt.

Heeft u de pretentie zich geroepen te voelen?
Laat het weten aan tile@scheldapen.be

IF YOU HAVE TO BE MONKEY
BE A MOTHING GORILLA

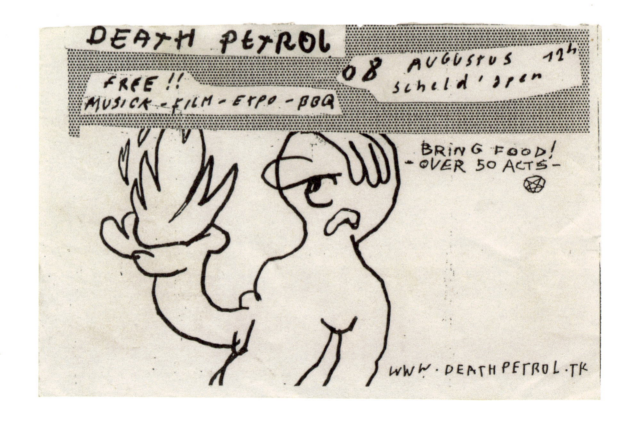

MUSICK - FILM - E

EEJTIES

donderdag 16 A

dj's

P

RO

IV

scheld'apen/d'

TECHNIKS JAN

GRATIS
T: 200

ERBOUVILLEKAAI, 36 APEN

JESUS CRÖST

VRIJDAG
21 APRIL 2000
20:00 PM

50 BEF

SCHELDA'PEN D'HERBOUVILLEKAAI 36
2020 ANTWERPEN

NO PASARAN 2

SKA

80'TIES

REGGAE

MOTOWN

& MORE

DJ. ZEN

+ too many shit DJ's

NO PASARAN 2

- SKA
- 80'TIES
- REGGAE
- MOTOWN
- & MORE

DJ. ZEN

+ too many shit DJ's

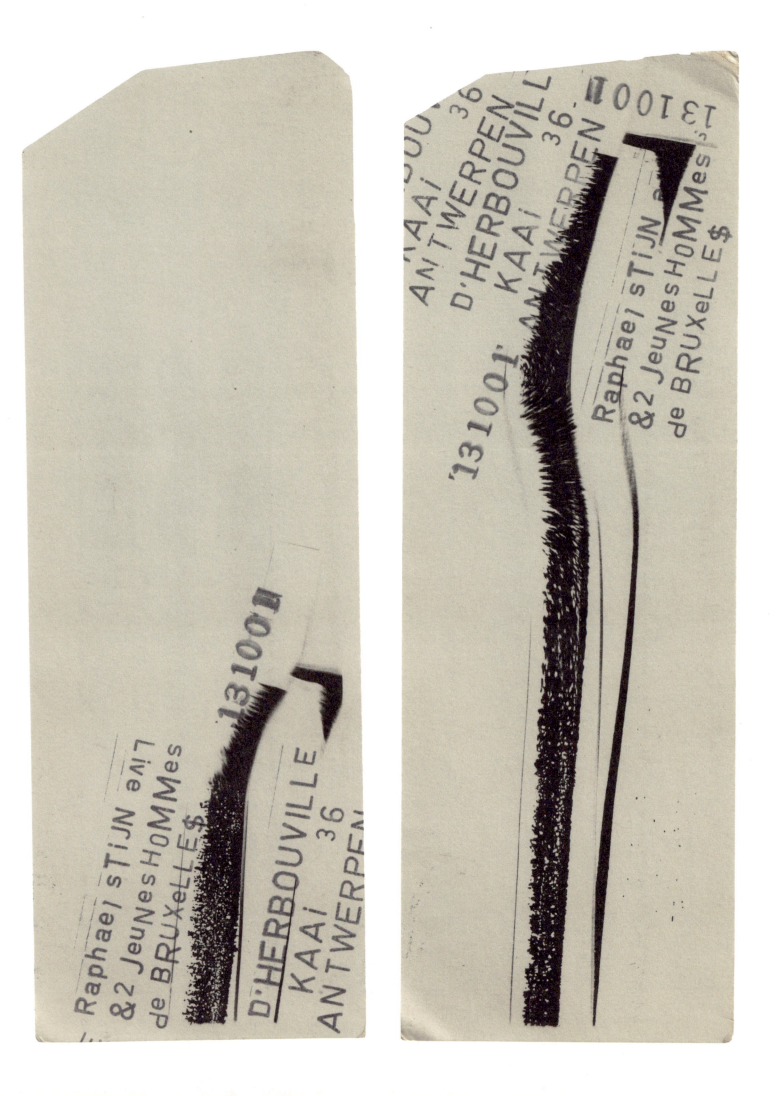

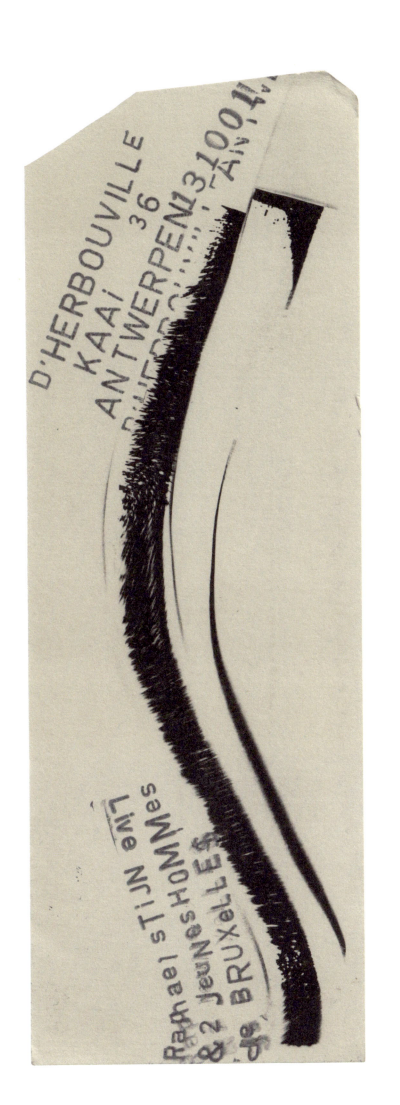
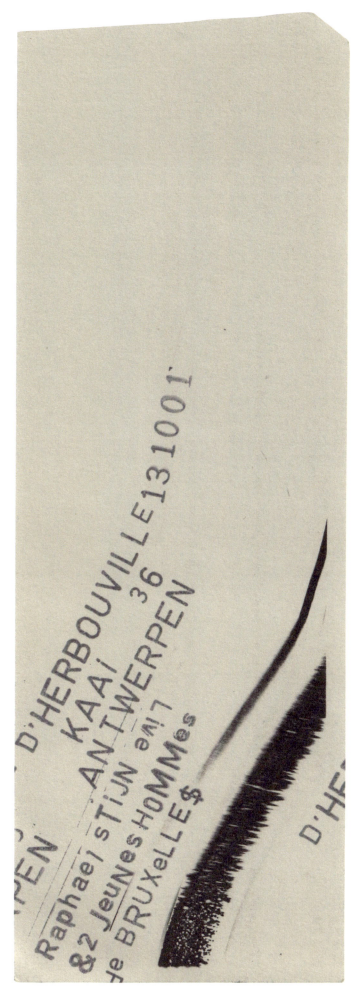

SCHELD'APEN
DECEMBER 2002

23/11
NACHT VAN DE MUZIKANT
ALLERLEI LOKALE SUPERHELD(INN)EN
DE GILL Z'N KEEL AL EEN KWARTEEUW DROOG
MEGA PARTY AAN DEN TOOG
DRESSCODE *LAS VEGAS
START: 23.00U

7/12
ATTACK/DECAY/SUSTAIN/RELEASE
LIVE ELECTRONICS WITH
Y'RI
DSR LINES
HALOFAUST
[ERZATZ]
START: 21.00U

14/12
BLAST

ONDERDAG 27 AUG	FRIJDAG 28 AUG	SATERDA 29 AUG
LA GRANDE BOUFFE	CABARET KAMIKAZE	SALON BOLIV
SCHELD APEN vzw	PAPEGAAIKE vzw	CAFE PRIV

SCHELD'APEN
NOVEMBER 2002

25/10
SPACE HUSTLERS
JRD (technoir – dosiz)
SOSVEN vs TOMISLAV (+16 – technoir)
STROHEIM (+16 – audiobot)
JAN TECHNIKS (beatscapes)
BOYTRONIK (neue weller)
audiobot@pandora.be or 0476 905 730
Starts at 22.00u!!

2/11
THE HUB
Avant-garde jazz trio from the Brooklyn underground scene ...Free jazz meets death metal inside the blades of a combine harvester
ONE LOUDER (o.v.)
A subtle and explosive cocktail
Starts at 20.30u!!

5/11
SCISSORFIGHT
This is how Motorhead, ZZTop and Antiseen sound if you jacked them up on steroids and LSD and handed them chainsaws and let them loose, Gladiator style...Acid Mountain Rock!
THE DUKES OF NOTHING
Members of Orange Goblin, Iron Monkey and Agrimony!
THE SEX MANIACS
X-members of Voorhees
Starts at 19.30u!

10/11
TOERISTENFEESTJE

23/11
NACHT VAN DE MUZIKANT
Al een kwart eeuw de Gill z'n keel droog!!

Elke Donderdag
VOLKSKEUKEN VANAF 19.00u!!!

D'Herbouvillekaai 36, 2020 Antwerpen
http://scheldapen.downfire.com
scheldapen@skynet.be

ZERO TOLERANCE
beats 'n pieces
SCARECROW
live breakbeat
HYSTERESIS
industrial dance music
start: 22.00u

20/12
VALINA (aus)
releaseparty 'vagabond', new LP/CD on Conspiracy Records
postrock, Shellac meets Fugazi
totally great!!!
start: 20.00u

Elke Donderdag
VOLKSKEUKEN VANAF 19.00u!!!

D'Herbouvillekaai 36, 2020 Antwerpen / scheldapen@skynet.be

SONDAG 30 AUG
SIESTA
ÎLE MOBILE vzw
Volledig verzorgde platte

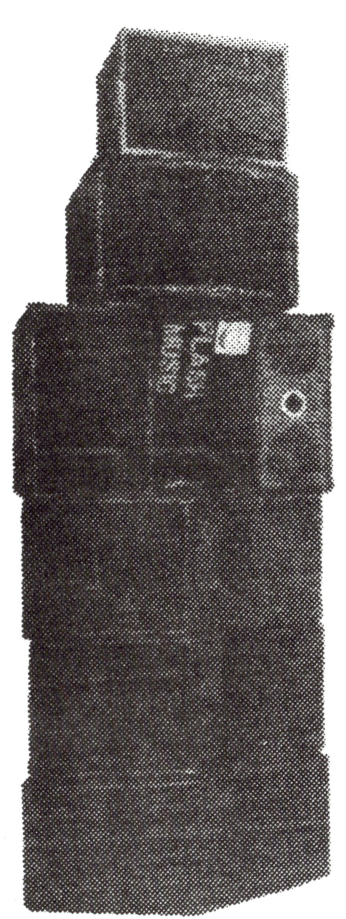

13/3/2010 20U

DE GELE NACHT LANG, MEER DAN 1000 VERSIES VAN DE TOPHIT **POPCORN**!! PRESENTATIE VAN EEN **POPCORN COVER COMPILATIE DUBBEL LP**!

MET:
DANIEL DE WERELDVERMAARDE BOTANICUS, MY LAND & LION, MAURO PAWLOWSKI, NIKÈ MOENS, VOM GRILL, DE LETTERLEGGERS, BENJAMIN VERDONCK, CIRCUS BULDERDRANG, WHITE CIRCLE CRIME CLUB, IDA MADONNA, DATASHOCK, CASA NERA, MIDNIGHT GALAXY, POSSESSED FACTORY, JOMMEKE GEERAERTS, LODE GEENS, FILIP VERVAET, KEVIN APETOWN, FLORIS VANHOOF, VINCENT STROEP, STROHEIM, W RAVENVEER, BUFFALO SIMON, FIA CIELEN, CHIEL VAN BERKEL, JESSIE SCHIETTECATTE, HEINI OBST, HANTRAX, REMÖRK, LUDO MICH, WOUT VERCAMMEN, CHRISTOPHE PIETTE, MICHIEL & STEVEN, NEL AERTS, BERT AERTS, RANI BAGERIA & HANNO SCHNEGG, F.L.U.T., FLEAMOUNTAINS, AUTISTIK YOUTH, MIAUX, FURNITURE CONVENTION, BISSY BUNDER
EN NOG VEEL MEER!!!

SCHELD'APEN, D'HERBOUVILLEKAAI 36, ANTWERP

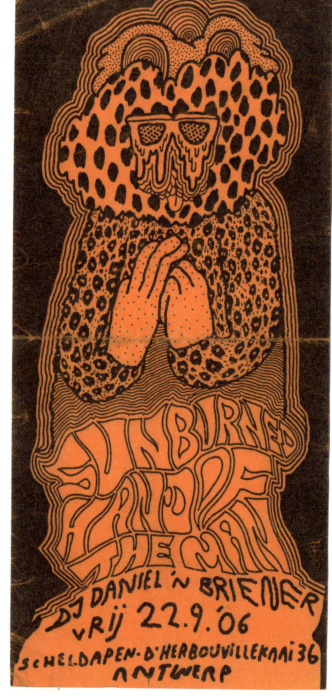

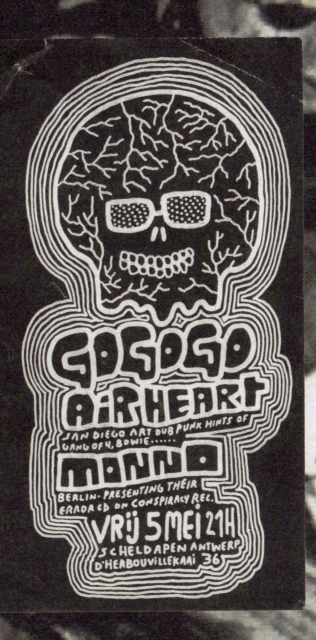

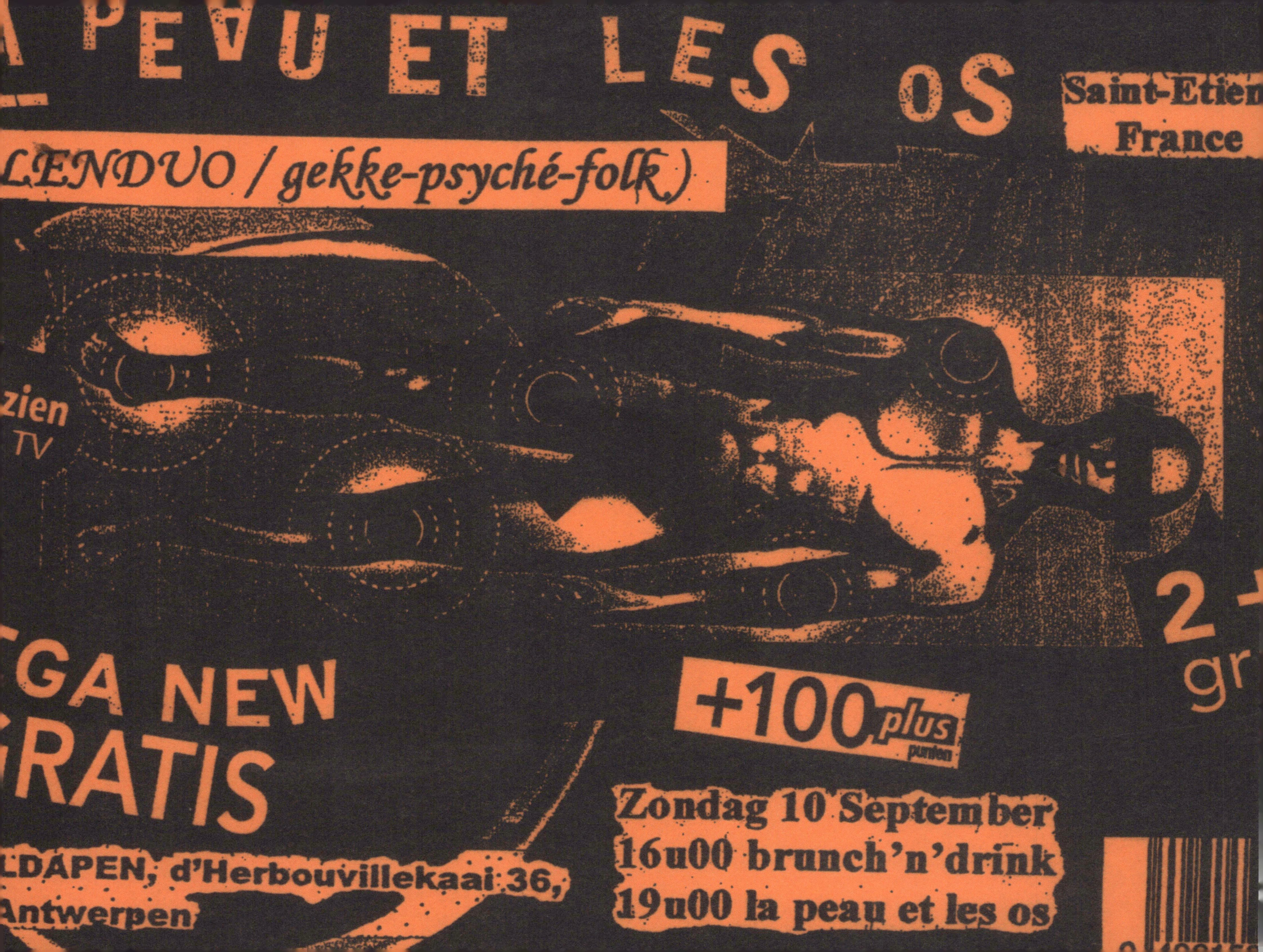

La peau et les os — Saint-Etienne, France

LENDUO / gekke-psyché-folk

+100plus punten

Zondag 10 September
16u00 brunch'n'drink
19u00 la peau et les os

GA NEW GRATIS

DAPEN, d'Herbouvillekaai 36, Antwerpen

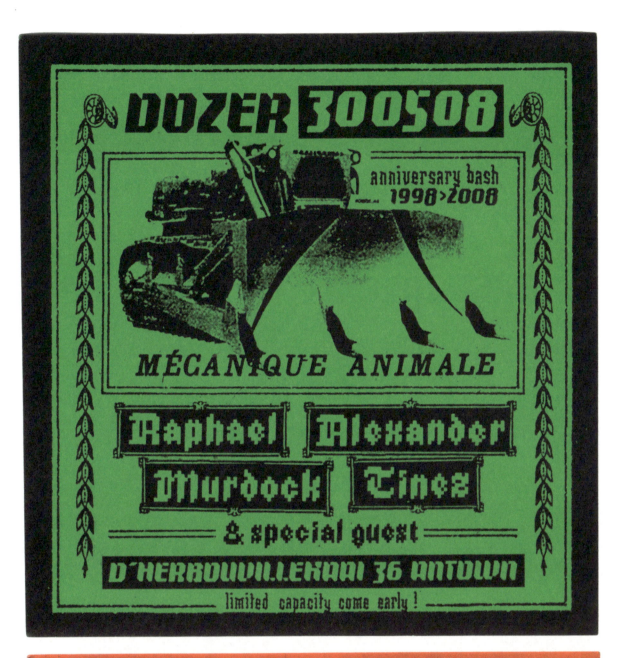

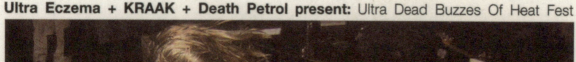

Ultra Eczema + KRAAK + Death Petrol present: Ultra Dead Buzzes Of Heat Fest

DARUMA T.

TEL. 00 32 (0)3 23

VRIJDAG 27 MEI, 21U: Cerberus Shoal (US), Monopolka (RUS), Mollenhauer (B), Cassis cornuta (B - presenting his new double CD on Ultra Eczema)
ZATERDAG 28 MEI, 16U: Smittekilde Expo (DEN - Trash silkscreened hardpop), Sickboy (B), Buffle (B), Butterknifekrush (GER), Holiday Pills (DEN), Porkchoco 'n Yoko Brieno (B) + DJ's Lamzak, Rotzak, Zeikzak.
S C H E L D A P E N • A N T W E R P E N
www.ultraeczema.com • www.kraak.net • www.deathpetrol.tk

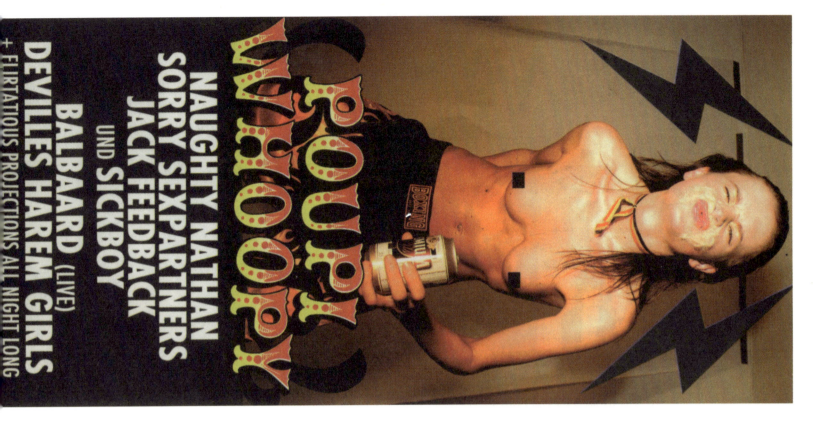
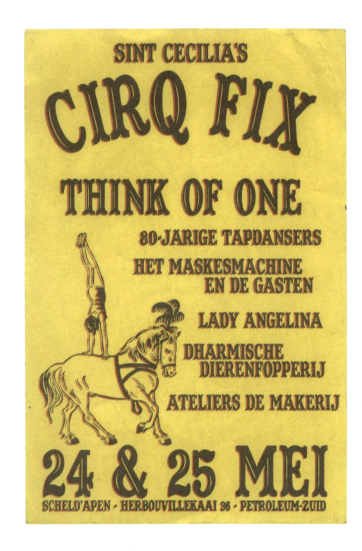

THE ILLEKTRO MOVEMENT IS UPPON US

15 JULI

DJ'S:
TechniksJan
Stroheim
3D Dance
8-O-freak

-> doors: 23u
-> Scheld'apen
   (d'herbouvillekaai)

1 €

MESSER CHUPS (ru)
surf-twang, electronische beats & theremins

DONDERDAG
08 JUNI 2006 **21u**
SCHELD'APEN
D'HERBOUVILLEKAAI 36 2020 ANTWERPEN

+ PSYCHOACOUSTIC GEOGRAPHERS (vs)
16mm psychedelische cinema

WWW.KONTRA.BE

2004 08 27 F · 2011 03 26 F · 2013 00 21 F

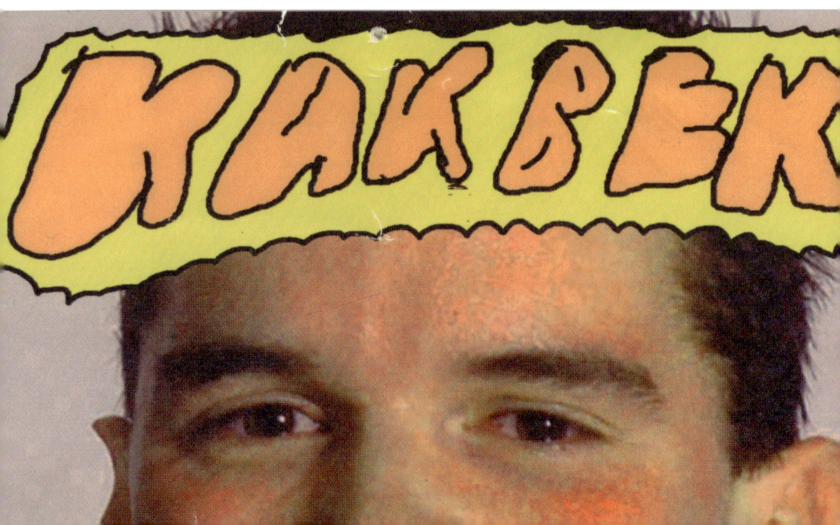

Vaillante
Racer (Rosso corsa records)
- CUPP CAVE
- Midnight Galaxy

dj's: Hugo Freegow
Paniekzaaier
BRAMOK
Die Hard 3-PAC

4 februari
scheldapen.be
myspace....

5€

VETTIG PATJE PRESENTEERT:

ZONDAG 21 JANUARI 2001

LESS
PUNK REGGAE (UK)
"...and I'll see you never work again" taunted Florence.

WITH MEMBERS FROM P.A.I.N. & HEADJAM

SCALE SHEER SURFACE (B)
DRUM 'N' BASS PUNKROCK

 **21.00 U AT SCHELD'APEN**
D'HERBOUVILLEKAAI 36 ANTWERPEN

VERBODEN AMOEDER MEE TE BRENGEN

FUIF

P chiro

19 JANUARI 2001
BIJ DE SCHELDA'PEN, 'D HERBOUVILLEKAAI 36
INKOM 100, VVK 80
START: 21 UUR
(BINNEN VOOR 23 UUR=GRATIS DRANKBON)

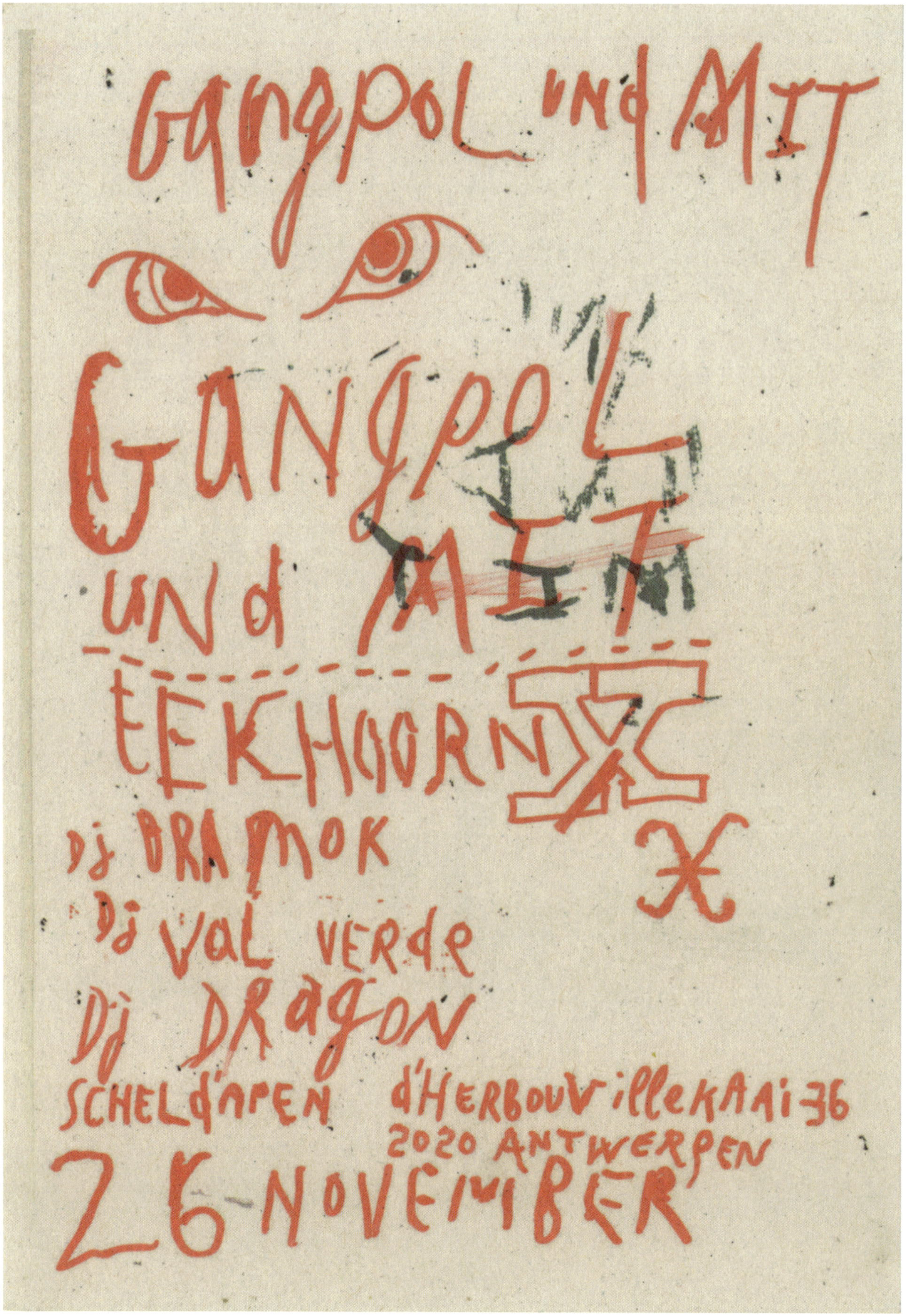

Gangpol und Mit

Gangpol und Mit

Eekhoorn

dj Dramok
dj Val Verde
dj Dragon

Scheldapen d'Herbouvillekaai 36
2020 Antwerpen
26 November

Full moon party

8 WEDNESDAY juli

– DJ BABA GOA TRANCE

– AND BEYOND...

Live acts +music
de walhala flashers
da wiz-stix playing with fire

BASS: THE FINAL FRONTIER...

2010 10 29 F • ›2008 04 19 F • ››2013 04 26 F

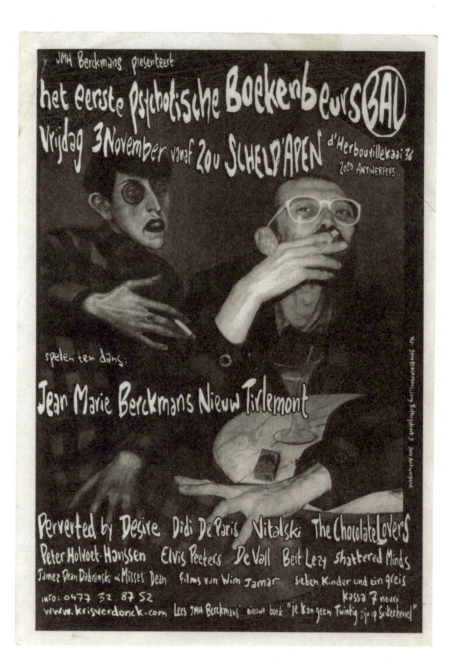

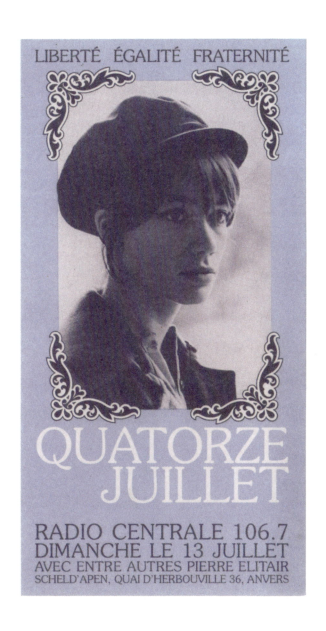

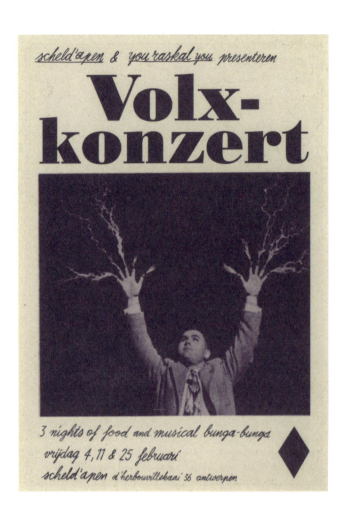

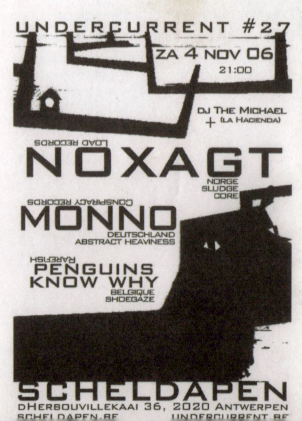

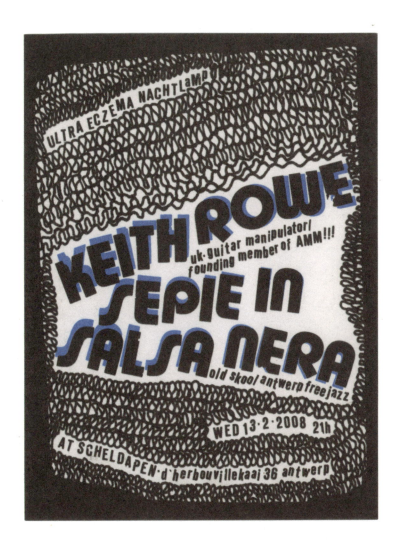

SCHELD'APEN OP DE BEURS!

4 & 5 MEI
9u - 16u
SJACHER-
BEURS

SCHELD'APEN OP DE BEURS!
4 en 5 MEI — 9u - 16u — SJACHERBEURS

Oude Vaartplaats 18 (Vogelmarkt), Antwerpen
www.scheldapen.be

MET o.a.
SCHELD'APEN RUILKAST/WISSELSTAND.
MAAKBA(A)R: HERSTELTOOG MET REMÖRK, MATTIAS CRE, SASKIA VAN DER GUGHT & VADER COSEMANS.
VOEDSELCOLLECTIEF DE BEEK INFOSTAND
BOEFBAAR DOOR KASPER DEVOS
SOLAR SHOP ZITHOEK
DE NACHTWINKEL
BILD UND STURM
BRIES
EXTRAPOOL/HALFWITHAL
HARMONIE
FABRIKAGE
HAARKAPSTER: TRUUS KEUSTERMANS
TAPESALE DISTRO (MET O.A KRAAK, BEYT-AL TAPES, SMELTKOP, TAPED SOUNDS, SLOOWTAPES, M+ TAPES, HARE AKEDOD, ..)
ULTRA ECZEMA'S MSS MEESTERD
FÜR DICH VERLAG
SHELDON SIEGEL'S GREVE TOTALE
NAOMI KOLSTEREN/STUDIO FLUIT
MAYKEN CRAENEN/HUIS HAAS
BARBARA VANDECAUTER
WANNES VERHEES
MAQUILLAGE: RENEE SIMONS
JON BIRDSONG
PLATENKRAAM IZJA RUTTEN
QUIET DAYS RECORDS
MINISTRY OF MASS
NARELLE DORE & SIGRID VOLDERS
JOHANNA TRUDZINSKI
WINNITRON SPELCONSOLE: THOMAS EN HANNES DE-VILLE
ZEEFDRUKATELIER: JELLE KINDT
APETOWN
TOPO COPY
ZINES
GRAFIEK
ZELFMAAK,
.....

Mensen! Dieren! Kinderen! Hier is het enigszins seizoensgebonden

SCHELD'APEN
EVENEMENTENOVERZICHT
Maart — April

IN DE *BETERE KRINGEN* OOK GEKEND ALS

SNEEUWKLOKJES & WINTERKONINCK
een Kroniek van Volharding

---

opgetekend door
LINKSHANDIGE PRIMATEN
met illustraties en
VERDUIDELIJKENDE GRAFIEKEN
en een voorwoord door
SCHIETER PAEPEN

---

geheel herziene druk verzorgd door
Afreux & Zoon
~ZELFWERKEND PATROONS~

---

voor Zaadlob en Stamper
voor Asfalt en Toendra
voor Antwerp en Beerschot

zitten wij goed in de Slappe Was & Warm onder de Wol in het Eengemaakte Koninkrijk

BELGIË
MMXI

Rest slechts te zeggen:
"REIK ONS DE SNEK EN WIJ ROEIEN!"
∞

ONS BLAZOEN: *EEN LOR*
ONS DEVIES: *HET LAM ZAL HEN WEIDEN*
ONS BROOD: *BELEGD*

Wendt u onbevreesd tot
~ WWW.SCHELDAPEN.BE ~
voor Verdere Verwarring.

Zoals steeds gedrukt door op Lederen Leest geschoeide Mathematici:
AVE DE WRIKKER, GRATIA PLENUS!

6,5%

DESTINATION EARTH

HIEROGLYPHIC BEING [US]
INNERCITY [BE]
HUNGRY SOUL [BE]

ZOOT RUFF SKI
COSMO KNOX
HANTRAX
RAPHAEL
HIELE

SUNDAY 8 SEPT
@SCHELD'APEN
D'HERBOUVILLEKAAI 50
2020 ANTWERPEN
8PM

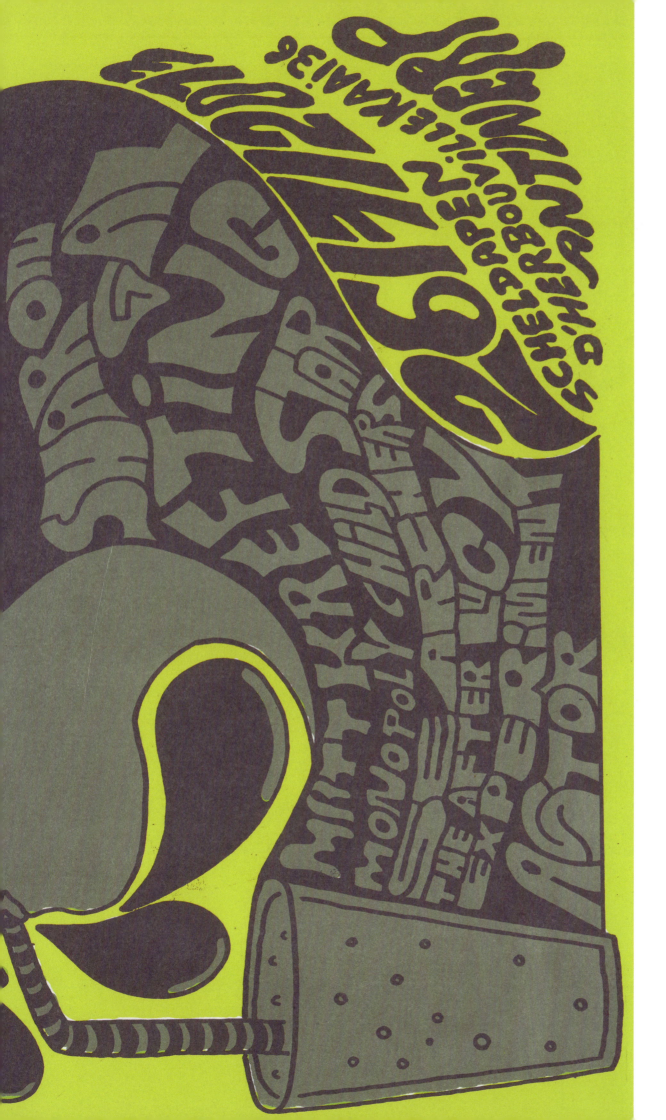

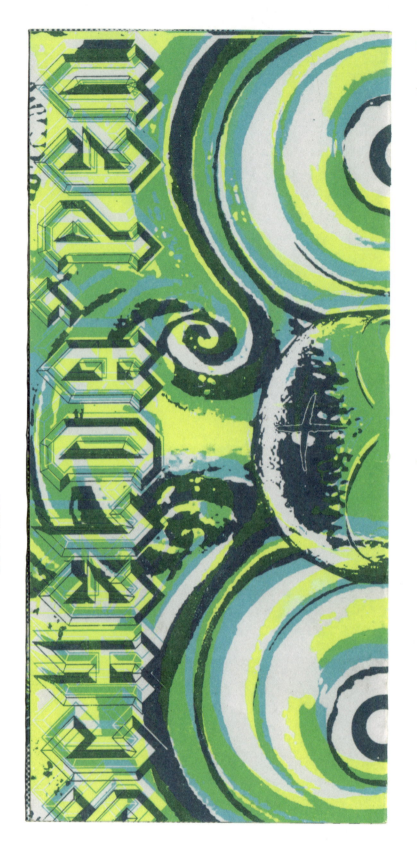

2006 02 PB • 2000 09 11 P

2006 02 PB • ›2002 12 14 F

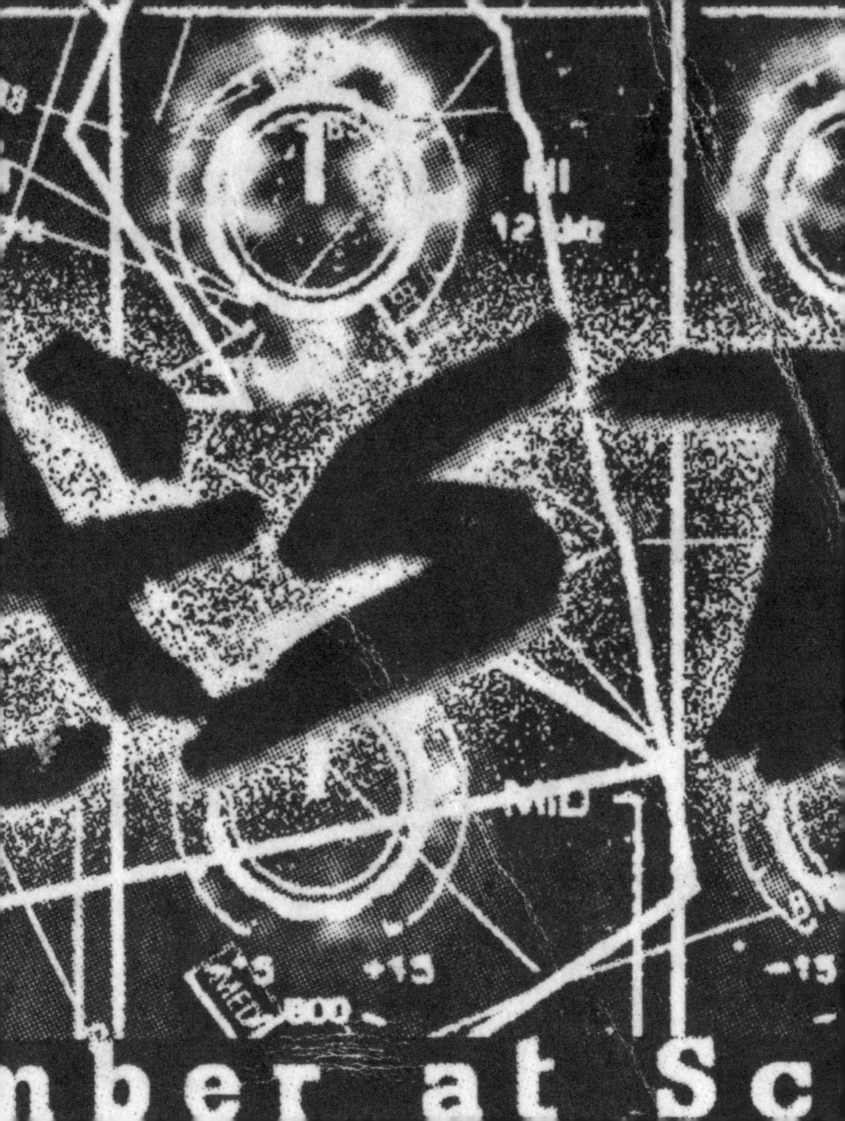

Heimatglück
(GERMAN DIRT)

30.000 Kollegen
(EX-AAK, GERMAN GODS!)

NO DOGS, NO MASTERS

20 NOV. 98
20.00 PM

150 - 200 BEF

SCHELDA'PEN D'HERBOUVILLEKAAI 36
2020 ANTWERP
NEAR FIETSERSTUNNEL

2001 04 14 F • ›2000 04 24 P • ››2002 06 15 P

DERITUX

SUCKS YOUR BOOZE

— IT'S YOUR SCE
SO FUCKI

AT: D'HERBOUVI

12 1OURE
START - 15:33
TILL BEDTIME
- 200 BF -

"SUPPORT IT-

SCHELD'APE
EKAAI 36 2000 ANTWERPEN

4 jaar 't pand

Schnap den hel
Help den kas
Scheepland
plaschende
Schedelpan
leep schand
scheelpand
na de schelp
Schand plee

scheld'apen

from dusk till da

2001 02 24 F • 2001 04 14 P • 2001 07 14 F • 2001 08 25 F

A Graphic Soil Sample
Roel Griffioen

GRAPHIC DESIGN of Scheld'Apen consciously is not an attempt to document the history of Scheld'Apen (1998-2013). The compilers did not try to extract a definitive story from the tasty but sometimes contradictory myths and legends that still surround Scheld'Apen, ten years after its closure. As the title suggests, this book focuses on the graphic work produced for the venue. The selected posters, flyers and program booklets are not chronologically arranged, but on visual grounds, sabotaging a historical reading of the material in advance. As readers, we are invited to be, first and foremost, viewers.

Leafing through the book, the viewer may also feel like a voyeur. This is because in some cases, we peer into the prehistory of now well-known artists' practices, looking at work that the creators themselves have outgrown. But also because there is something paradoxical about the aestheticization of the work on display. This has to do with its curious status as applied art – creative publicity material for a subcultural entertainment venue. The fate of a flyer was to end up crumpled at the bottom of your backpack or folded in a trouser pocket. And a concert poster's natural habitat was a smeared toilet door. (The tape ends and spray paint on some of the posters remind us of this humble habitat.) For this book, they have been pressed against a scanner window in all their nakedness, to be served high-res to our hungry eyes, in a way that feels both delightful and slightly uncomfortable. In a weighty coffee table book, no less.

Specifically as an outsider – I know Scheld'Apen only from its lore – I am inclined to see the graphic work in this book not as graphic work only. It is too tempting to look for visual traces of the history of its place of origin – to read the book as a kind of soil sample that reveals the different sediments that have formed there. The idea behind this is that the graphic expressions of Scheld'Apen did not arise in a vacuum. Perhaps they reveal something about the changing networks that came together here, about a changing way of programming, about changing budgets, changing printing methods, changing audiences, even a changing relationship with the outside world?

The story of Scheld'Apen begins in June 1998, when a group of young people squats a vacant canteen for railway employees. The building is sandwiched between a garbage dump and the last functioning installations of Petrol-Zuid – once the heart of the petrochemical port industry, but at the end of the twentieth century a neglected and polluted piece of post-industrial wasteland next to the river Scheldt. The birth of an "artistic sanctuary" (artistieke vrijplaats) is announced to the municipality and the press by fax. The municipal council takes a fairly accommodating stance. A reasonable rental contract is worked out, and Scheld'Apen is silently tucked away in an annex of the youth policy.

On the earliest posters and flyers unearthed by Benny Van den Meulengracht-Vrancx and Bent Vande Sompele, you'll find exactly the xeroxed crust-rustic insane graphics, interspersed with squatting and anarchy signs, that you'd expect from a squat from this period (in this case a tolerated former squat with a rental agreement). There are vomiting mythical creatures, bleeding penises, degenerate Suskes and Wiskes (lots of Wiskes especially) or a Flemish core family adorned with Hitler mustaches and swastikas. There are benefits for animal rights and for an Antifa activist in custody. In this early material, Scheld'Apen is not yet consistently called Scheld'Apen, but for example Scheldesquat, Spauwsquad, Het Kraakpand or simply Het Pand.

After the turn of the century, more color appears in the publicity material. There is a lot of screen printing – by art students using the facilities at the academy, I was told. The squatting rhetoric slowly disappears from view. Explicitly political posters and flyers are still present, but limited to the punk shows organized by one Vettig Patje. In any case, it is clear that during this period, different groups or scenes program in Scheld'Apen, all of which take care of their own publicity. On flyers for ska, reggae, electro or goa-trance nights, you will find all the visual motifs you would expect from those subcultures. This multiplicity of voices does not always make for visually interesting graphics. But perhaps it does foreshadow the modus operandi of Het Bos, the place in which Scheld'Apen incarnated: a cultural center with a clearly distinct character and identity of its own, but simultaneously an open infrastructure that can be used by others.

From about 2003 or 2004 on, a new centripetal force is visible in the graphic expressions of Scheld'Apen. Not coincidentally, this is also a phase of organizational stabilization and cautious professionalization. Simple agreements are made, for example the decision that all bar revenue is for the house and the entrance fee for the artists. In 2005, Scheld'Apen is recognized by the Province of Antwerp as a regional youth house and a small subsidy is approved, which makes for more available publicity resources. There is a more regular collaboration with a handful of designers, bringing a few distinct signature styles to the fore. Despite the mutual differences, the tone is often the same: rather in-crowd, rarely serious, generally absurd and contrarian. Filth with flair, to express it in alliterative Suske and Wiske-terms (where did Wiske go, by the way?). Shit, puke and deformed genitalia remain popular themes, but technically as well as visually the material does become fuller, fatter, weirder, Scheld'Aperier.

Is it correct to state that the general picture later on – say, from 2007 – becomes more differentiated again? The pool of artists and designers who produce publicity material is growing. The visual work made during this phase contains collages, staged photos, cardboard tableaux and other homecrafted treats. The absurdism remains, but the creepy horniness and fecal humor subtly fade into the background. The programming also becomes broader, giving more attention to theatre, dance, film and literature. Also, the Scheld'Apen family tree seems to spawn various new offshoots: initiatives, publications, festivals, spaces and labels that operate partly within and partly outside the mothership. Yet the moment the philosophy of self-organization, niche programming and general experimentation takes root in more and more places in the city, the continued existence of Scheld'Apen on the quay is no longer a given. Of all development plans projected for this location, the one for which Scheld'Apen eventually has to make way is the most off-the-wall: a joint football stadium for sworn arch enemies Royal Antwerp and Beerschot. Scheld'Apen closes its doors at the end of 2013, to reopen in early 2014 as Het Bos, in a much larger building on the other side of the city center.

    The microhistory of Scheld'Apen fits – I think – into a larger story about subcultural centers and their changing place in the city. Seeing the word 'autonomous' on one of the first flyers reminds me of concepts such as the 'Temporary Autonomous Zone' (T.A.Z.) and 'terrain vague' that circulated in the more artistic parts of the squatting movement during the 1990s and early 2000s. Both terms – the T.A.Z. and the terrain vague – concern the unauthorized appropriation of residual spaces in the folds and creases of a political-economic system that strives for totality. These spaces can be temporarily appropriated by, for example, marginal groups "before local authorities get a grip on them with their regulatory greed", as philosopher and jurist Marc Schuilenburg later summarized. And it is precisely in these spaces, located in a clandestine twilight zone outside the formal circuits of art, politics and society, that intense flare-ups of creativity, experimentation and energy arise. Or so the story went.

    It is no coincidence that Scheld'Apen announced itself to the outside world as an "artistic sanctuary" (artistieke vrijplaats), after the squatting took place. The English 'sanctuary' does not fully cover the Dutch word vrijplaats – which translates literally as 'free-place' or 'freezone'. The word was popular at the time, because it evoked an image of an autonomous pirate state where the rules and bourgeois morals of 'ordinary' society did not apply. That pirate romance camouflaged the fact that, like Scheld'Apen, most productive and lasting sanctuaries were actually involved in a constructive dialogue with the municipality (or at least sympathetic officials or aldermen), local residents, utility companies, and so on. This constructive dialogue with the world beyond the proverbial pirate island was accompanied by a constant and sometimes very fervent internal conversation about principles and pragmatism, about freedom and dependence – in short, about how far this courtship with the outside world should go.

This book contains posters that aim to be transgressive and contrarian, while the logo of the city of Antwerp appears in the lower right corner. This dialectic is illustrative of the relative autonomy of the generation of sanctuaries to which Scheld'Apen belongs – places that navigate between a lofty autonomy ideal and a pragmatic Realpolitik. Still, it seems that Scheld'Apen managed to find that sweet spot between visibility and invisibility, between recognition and denial, between daylight and underground. It did not turn into a Trojan horse for gentrification – perhaps because of its peripheral location at the time (today, the city has grown considerably bigger). Neither did it become a flagship project for Flemish youth policy. And there was never anyone gazing over the programmers' shoulders.

    Perhaps this is a good time to seriously consider what kind of place Scheld'Apen was. Not only because it has been ten years since the building was vacated, but also to think about what conditions are necessary for these kinds of places to emerge and exist. The circumstances seem to get increasingly more unfavourable. Just think of the criminalization of squatting in many European countries, the emergence of an anti-squatting industry, the insight among policymakers that temporary experimental or countercultural places can be instrumentalized in urban renewal programmes, raging gentrification, city marketing, the financialization of housing, and so on. In the Netherlands, squat hagiographies are regularly published, in which the disappearance of frayed edges, artistic sanctuaries or even the counterculture in general is lamented. Even though that may be an exaggeration, it is clear that most folds and creases have been ironed out of cities, making it increasingly difficult for bottom-up initiatives to take root.

    In Belgium, the circumstances seem less dramatic at first glance. As a sometime resident and frequent passer-by in Antwerp, I have always envied the fact that during the past decade, there have consistently been two or three (temporary) stopping places of overlapping art and music scenes in Antwerp – places such as Pink House, Forbidden City, Stadslimiet, Samenschool or toitoiDROME, and probably many more. Small but sometimes surprisingly international hubs for creative experimentation. Places not planted by policymakers, but emerging from individuals, collectives or scenes. Yet there are signs that, also in Antwerp and other Belgian cities, free space is shrinking or even becoming finite. During the last years that I lived in Antwerp, there were many complaints about how the city branded certain places as 'image-lowering' (imagoverlagend) or as causing nuisance. The infrastructure of existing institutions and initiatives is under pressure from cultural cutbacks at various political levels. Also striking is the fact that in recent years, a number of symposia, biennales and art productions in Belgium have paid attention to topics such as gentrification, artwashing and lack of space. I am thinking, for example, of the 'Gentrify Everything' edition of the Borgerhout gallery biennale Borg in 2016; the participatory theater play CC De Vleeshaak about the gentrification of the Antwerp abattoir quarter Den Dam (Peter Boelens, Carl Cappelle and Sara Dandois, 2019); the film WTC A Love Story (Wouter de Raeve and Lietje Bauwens, 2020) about vacancy management and gentrification in the Brussels North quarter, and the Kunstenpunt-initiated research project 'Ruimte voor kunst' ('Space for art') in 2020.

  Intentionally or not, this book proves to me the enduring power of places on the fringes of city policy – places that are shaped from the bottom-up, and don't have to take the logic of the market or mainstream culture into account. The fact that so much book-worthy graphic work has been produced here is also a testament to the value of a place where artists and experimental designers can develop in a relatively sheltered environment – or technicians, treehouse builders, beer pourers and pizza bakers, for that matter. A place without formal structure, lacking explicit rules or clear-cut roles, where simply trying out something is accepted.

  Still, it fits GRAPHIC DESIGN of Scheld'Apen that it refuses to be a nostalgic book. Indeed, I get the feeling that Scheld'Apen was never a nostalgic place. If it was faced with a threat of closure, a good closing party was organized – and if that closure then failed to materialize, a reopening party. This would be followed by a continued cheerful construction of "the most unclean youth culture temple of the Low Lands", to quote one of the program booklets. Another booklet reads: "The sky is the limit. But we aim higher." Let's hope that in the coming decades, countless youth culture temples will aim for the sky and higher in Antwerp and beyond. Places that are completely different in form and target group, but all equally unclean, reckless, exuberant and noisy.

BITLORD.COM PROGRAM

ISOHUNT.COM
TORRENTSPY.COM
PIRATEBAY.COM

ELKE DONDERDAG JONG

WORKSHOP: ZELF JONGLEER GERIEF MAKEN

ORIGINAL SCHELD'AP

Ateliers ALEX HOENIG S.14.

NATUURLIJK MEE LEREN JONGLEREN: M

..ERE, TS 20-22U D'HERBOUVILLE-KAAI 35 ANTWERPEN

ANDERS MAKEN - WE IETS - PROBEER ZELF IETS MEE TE NEMEN

...ALLEN, KEGELS, DIABOLO, DEVILSTICK,......

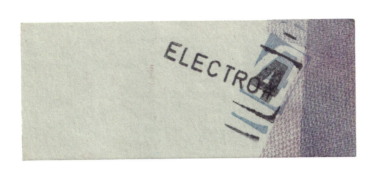

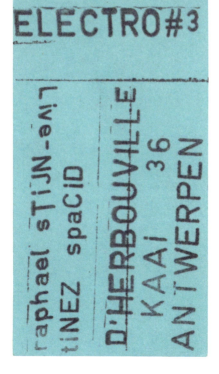

2001 08 25 F · 2001 10 13 F · 2002 03 02 F · 2002 05 25 F · 2001 04 14 F · 2001 07 14 F

VISIONS OF WAR... (U.K.) (LOCAL DISCO HEROES)

SYC (HEAVY BLACK METAL SCREAMS)

30 AUG. 150,-
HERBOUVILLEKAAI 36
ANTWERP (NEAR FIETSERSTUNNEL...)

SHOWS START WHEN IT'S DARK AND IF IT'S HOT IT'S IN THE GARDEN..... DRINX ARE CHEAP AND VEGAN FOOD WANTS YOU TO EAT HIM...

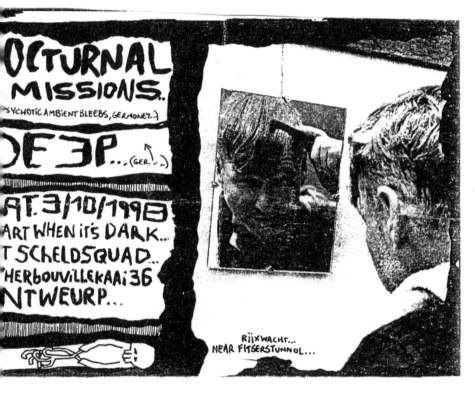

NOCTURNAL MISSIONS.. (PSYCHOTIC AMBIENT BLEEBS, GERMONEY...)

DEEP... (GER...)

SAT. 3/10/1998
START WHEN IT'S DARK...
AT SCHELDSQUAD...
D'HERBOUVILLEKAAI 36
ANTWEURP...

RIJXWACHT... NEAR FITSERSTUNNOL...

PLACEBO... SEIZED...

BOTH BANDS COME FROM CANADA.. PLACEBO PLAYS MOODY & CATCHY TO CRAZY NEUROTIC PUNKROCK... AND I DON'T KNOW WHAT SEIZED IS PLAYING... COME CHECK IT TOGETHER WITH THE USUAL VEGIE FOOD, ANTWERP ARROGANCE AND

+ **STHRALER 80** (GERMAN GREAT PO)

SUN. 4.10.1998 AROUND 20.00...
75,- ENTRANCE... AT
SCHELD'ASQUAD...
D'HERBOUVILLEKAAI 36
ANTWERP
NEAR FIETSERSTUNNEL

DON'T BRING YER DOGS... THEY HEAR 8 TIMES BETTER THEN WE DO AND THEY DON'T LIKE THE MUSIC

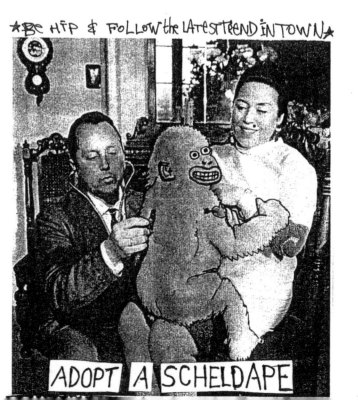

★BE HIP & FOLLOW THE LATEST TREND IN TOWN★

ADOPT A SCHELDAPE

ALCATRAZ (EMOJAZZHARDCOREPØNK UIT FRANKRIJK...)

LISELOTTE (PUNK SWITSERL.)

+ **ONE BAND MORE**

DO. 17 SEPTEMBRE 199
AROUND 20.00 Ó CLOCK...
D'HERBOUVILLEKAAI 36
ANTWERP
NEAR RIJXWA
FITSERSTU

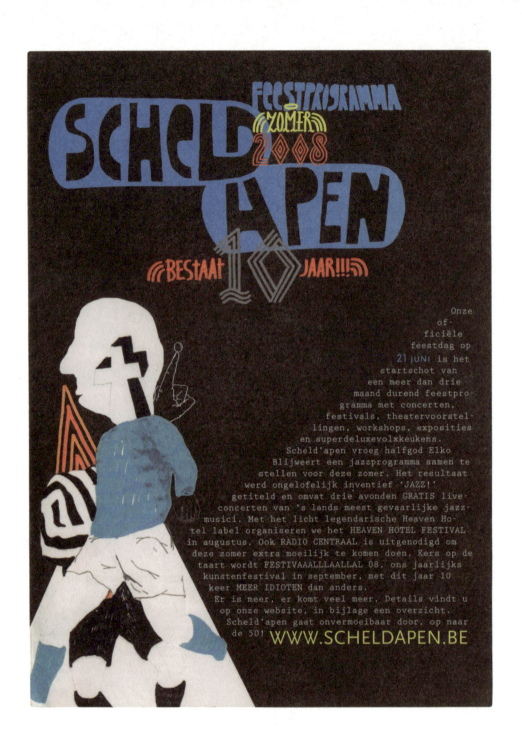

«2009 11 29 F • ‹1998 09 17 F • 2008 06 PB • 2005 12 15 F

Onze officiële feestdag op 21 JUNI is het startschot van een meer dan drie maand durend feestprogramma met concerten, festivals, theatervoorstellingen, workshops, exposities en superdeluxevolkkeukens. Scheld'apen vroeg halfgod Elko Blijweert een jazzprogramma samen te stellen voor deze zomer. Het resultaat werd ongelofelijk inventief 'JAZZ!' getiteld en omvat drie avonden GRATIS live-concerten van 's lands meest gevaarlijke jazz-musici. Met het licht legendarische Heaven Hotel label organiseren we het HEAVEN HOTEL FESTIVAL in augustus. Ook RADIO CENTRAAL is uitgenodigd om deze zomer extra moeilijk te komen doen. Kers op de taart wordt FESTIVAAALLLAALLAL 08, ons jaarlijks kunstenfestival in september, met dit jaar 10 keer MEER IDIOTEN dan anders. Er is meer, er komt veel meer. Details vindt u op onze website, in bijlage een overzicht. Scheld'apen gaat onvermoeibaar door, op naar de 50! WWW.SCHELDAPEN.BE

Tijdens een waterschaarste in Tapei, de hoofdstad van Taiwan, word pornoacteur Hsiao-Kang verliefd op Shiang-chyi, werkzaam in een porno videotheek. De film wisselt pornografische scenes af met muzikale intermezzo's (chinese pop songs uit de jaren '60) en bevat amper dialoog. Dit geeft vaak een komisch effect, maar alle gelach zal uiteindelijk verstommen.

The Wayward Cloud [TIAN BIAN YI DUO YUN]
Tsai Ming-liang| 2005| Taiwan| 114'
donderdag 15 december 2005
Kontra vzw
Scheld'apen
d'Herbouvillekaai 36
2020 Antwerpen.

deuren 20.30
film start ± 21.00!!!

160

HEROPENING
25 MAART 2005
ELKE VRIJDAG VOLKKEUKEN VANAF 19U / ELKE ZATERDAG KONTRA-CINEMA + INTERNETCAFE VANAF 19U
SCHELD'APEN
D'HERBOUVILLEKAAI 36-2020 ANTWERPEN-WWW.SCHELDAPEN.BE

2005 03 PB

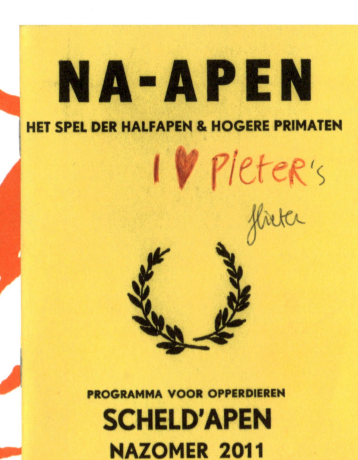

ua it (Moscow)

wadadakwa

tor presenteert:

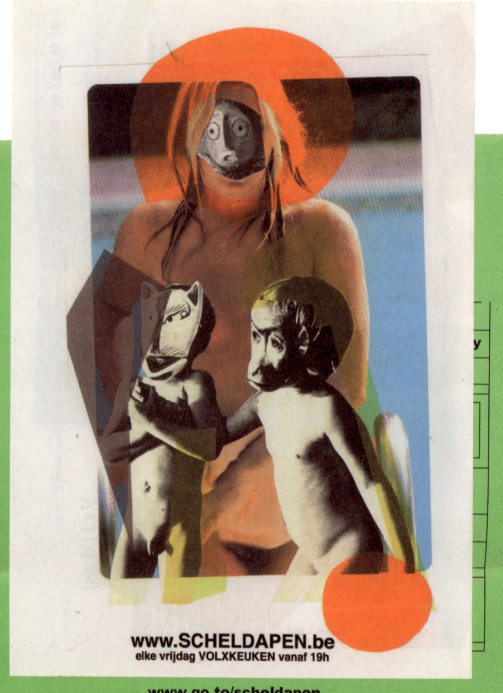

www.SCHELDAPEN.be
elke vrijdag VOLXKEUKEN vanaf 19h

www.go.to/scheldapen
ELKE dONDERdAG OpEn BAR + VegeTaRIES eten VANAF 7uur
(coming soon LuXe-volXkeuke...)

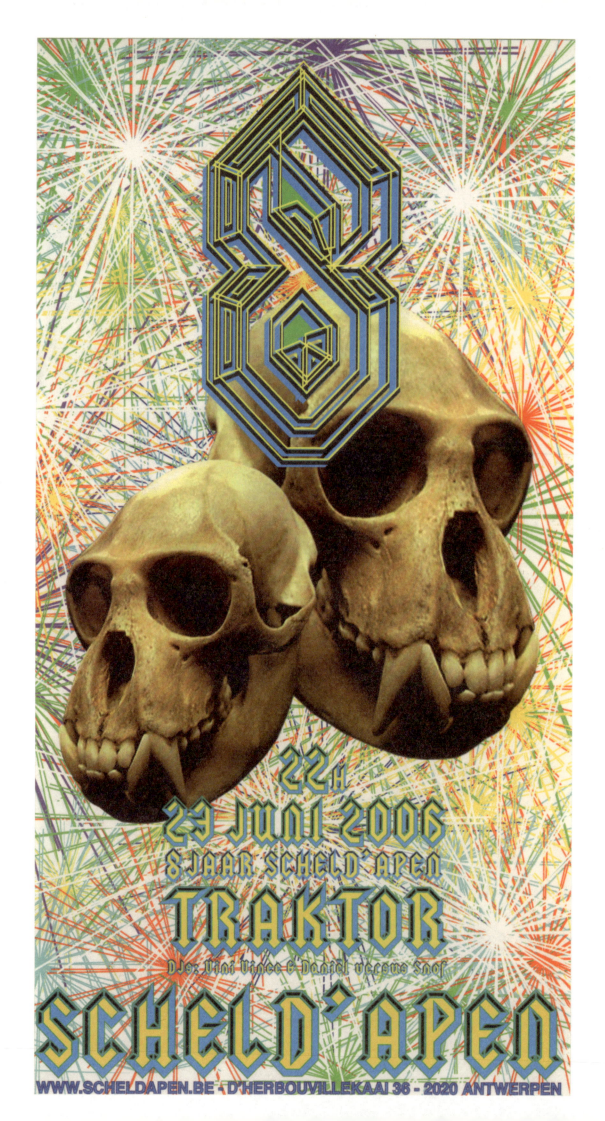

Gilles' birthday PARTY
ZAT. 25 NOV. '00
heksen & vampieren
feest. Be dressed!!
at Scheld'apen
d'Herbouvillekaai 36
2000 Antwerpen

Don 11/5/2000 23:00

bassdrum Jr.

- Dirk De Laet — bass
- Tamer Kaya — drums
- Peppi Pepermans — sax
- Merlin — mix

**SCHELDE A'PEN PRESENTEERT:
BASSDRUM JR (concert)
+ AFTER PARTY (DJ Marie Antoinette)
D'Herbouvillekaai 36   2020 Antwerpen**

ARRRR

SAIL!!!

X WARD ZWART BRECHT VDB FUNERAL FOLK
CRAMA EN VRIENDENBOEL APETOWN STELLA
DS EN DE GILLES AAN DEN TOOG ME ROMMEL
DA HIER AL JAREN LIGT EN WEG MOT!!!!

SAIL!!!

LDAPEN.BE → D'HERBOUVILLEKAAI 36 ANTWERPEN

13 AUG.

AT THE SCHELDA PEN

HERBOUVILLEKAAI 36/ANTWERP

X-MAS T...

Winniema...
Far W...
Civalizee...
High Gr...

22/12

Kra...

D" Here...

Ant...

Gate Pressure : 100 BEF

SURIFOOD
Verbondstraat 58
03 / 288 62 51

Cocktailbar

Cool Runnings

Leopoldplaats 9   Antw...

ME A COME

turing

...Sound (NL)
...st Crew
...Foundation
...ade Sound

@

...akpand
...uvillekaai
...werpen

Doors : 10 PM

g.baeck
Brood en Banket
Wittestraat 80
2020 Antwerpen
Tel.: 03 237 82 33

come early

PARTY TIME AGAIN

KI PROMOTIONS & GAMORAH

SAT. 15 O

BOOTC

GAMORAH

3 MAJOR. Mc E

AUTONOOM JEUGDCENTRUM AT H

...OUND PROUDLY PRESENTS

...4.2000

...mp II

SOUND

...ONY PANZAR

...BOUVILLEKAAI ANTWERPEN

2000 04 15 P

Lijn nr. ....

Aankondiging		BROERTJES DOEN E...
Nr.¹	Aard	EN
		STEFFI
		STEVEN DE P...
Aankondiging		
		RAPHAEL ANTWERPEN
		ANTON PRICE
Nr.	Uur	
95	240201	D'HERBOUVILLE
79		

Nr.

Ⓑ

Spoor 8

ELECTRO FEEST 1	Antwoord		
UIT AMSTERDAM	Aard	Nr.	Uur
STIJN ONCERT BO888	Doorzending van de aankondiging		Uur van doorrit
	Nr.	Uur	
96	240201		

2001 02 24 P

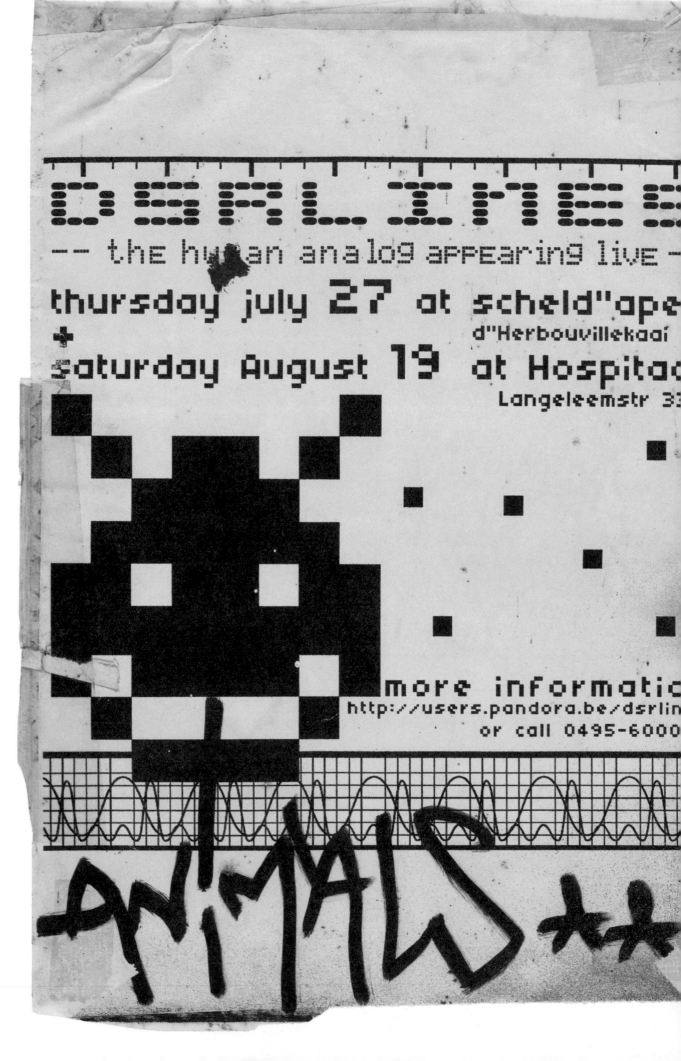

			kHz
ZION LIONS	ROOTS BAMBU SOUND	CRUCIAL P	METER kHz
CHELD'APEN	PRESENTS : BLUE MOUNTAIN PEAKS		STATION MHz
D'HERBOUVILLEKAAI 36, NAAST PETROL			CHANNEL
8.DEC.2006	ENTRÉE: €3	DOORS: 22.00H	LINEAR MHz
			BAND

20061208F

Dylan Murdock Shorty Soi
HOSTED BY MC RICKY D

DRUM n BASS

D' HERBOUVILLEKAAI 36
SCHELDA'PEN

28/07/Y2K+1

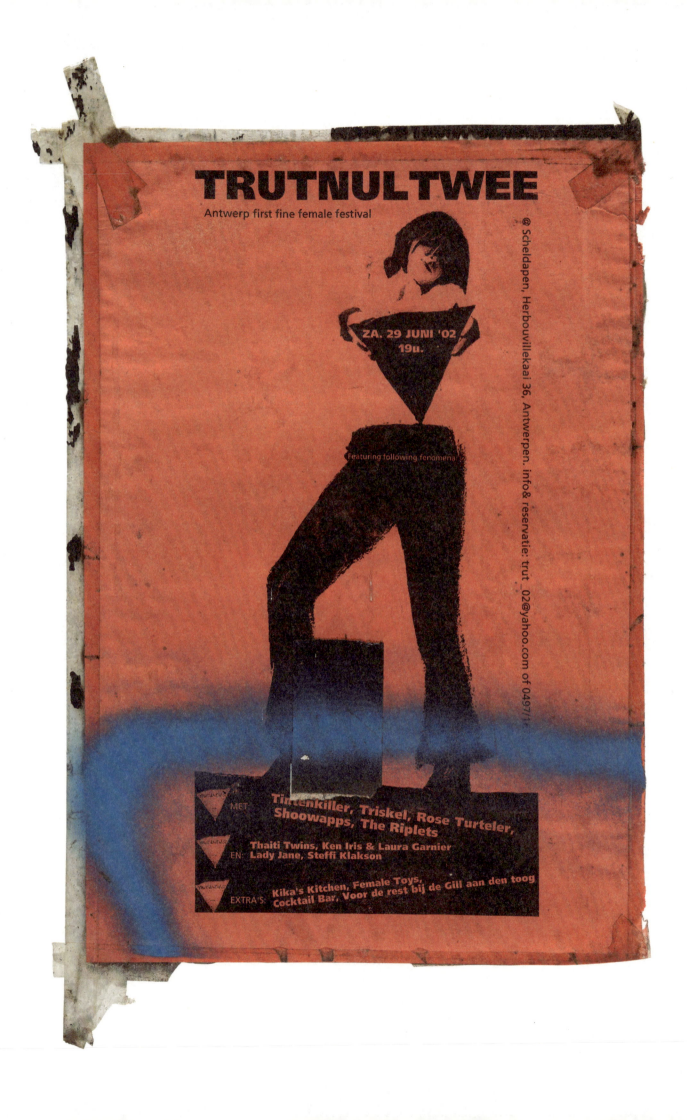

electro **FUNK** breaks

funk

ELECTRIC SUPPLIERS
TECHNIKS JAN
PHILIP ■ ORG

ATOMIC

Cragstan

design by primastyle

damage:
4 euro

BABES FROM RUSSIA
BABSEY
GROUPOS CHICAS
ANN CHRISTY

Speed

tra... try out met ha...
Sa... internationals

fre... oncert 29 mei
SCHELD APE

subdeviant night!
22 sept.

cassini
house of lov

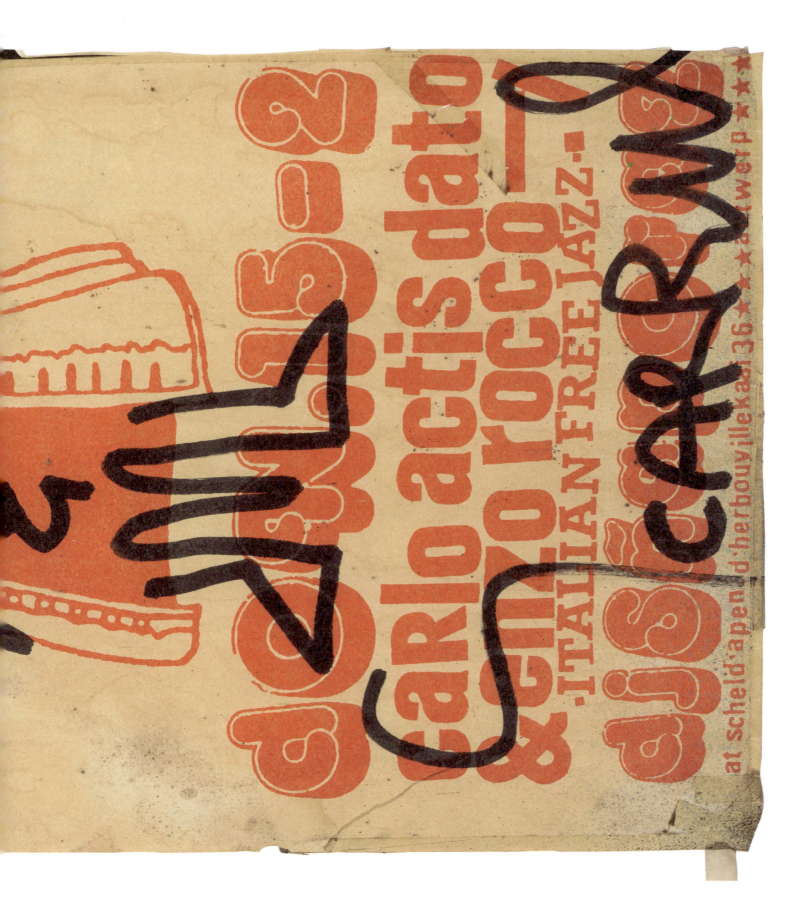

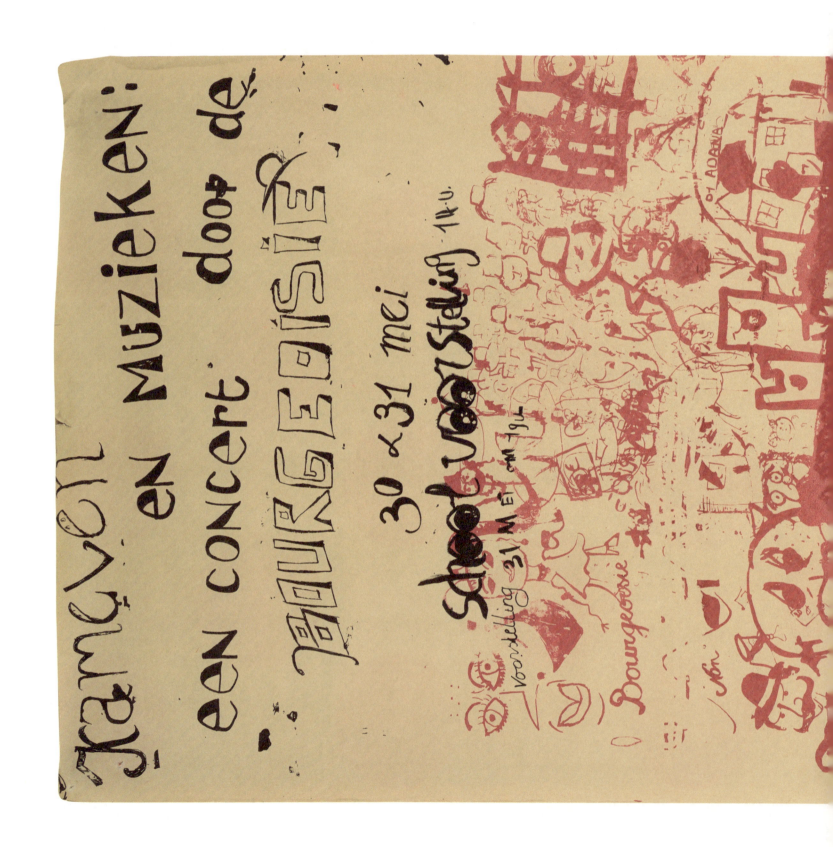

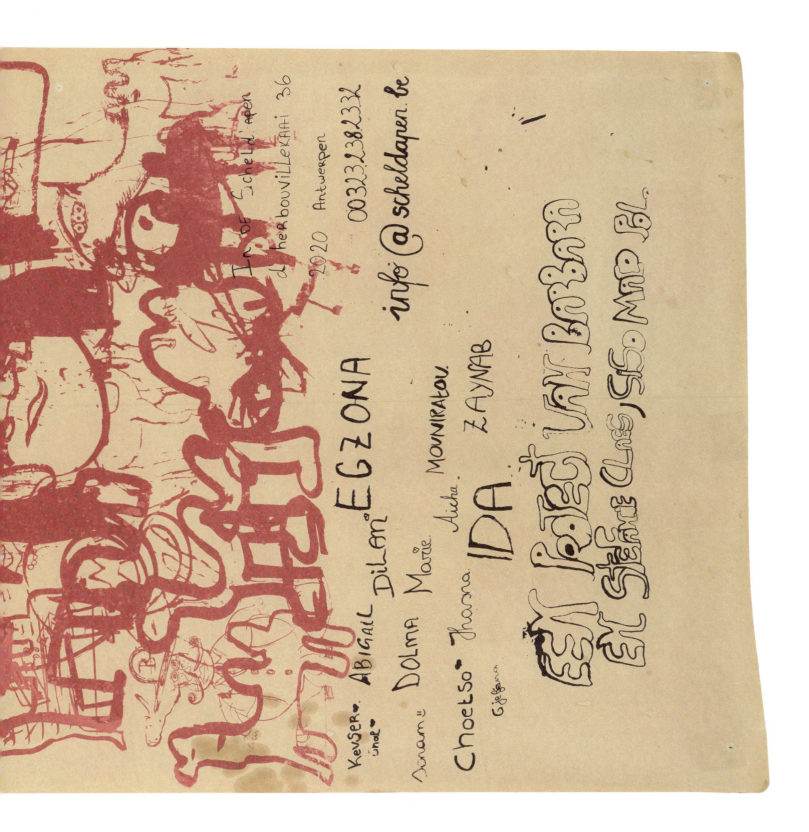

le quatorze ju[illet]
de radio cen[tre]
à partir de l'après-midi dans
le 13 juillet

dj pierre élitaire dj maladie d[…]
scheld'apen 36 quai d'herbouville […]
émissions directes sur le 103.9 fm […]

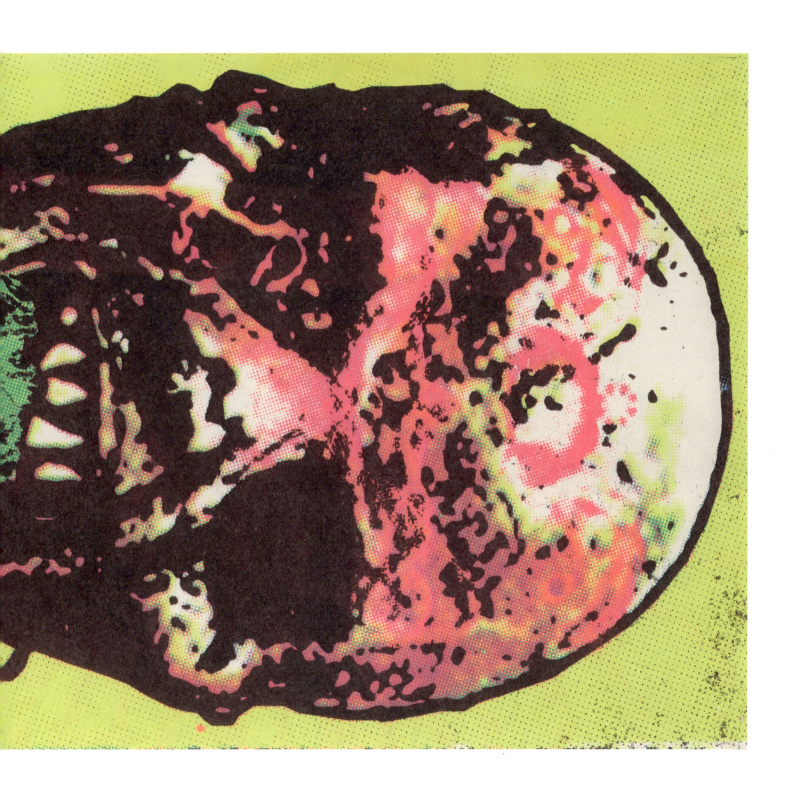

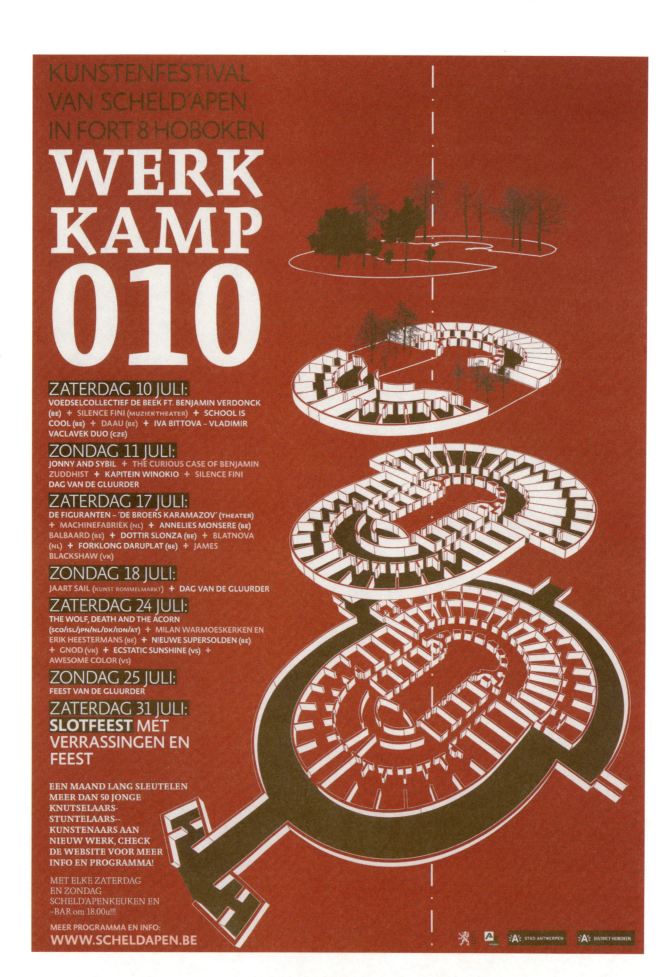

2006
02
PB

Voorzitter, secretaris, penningmeester en de voltallige ledenraad van de Organisatie ter Bevordering van Volksverheffing en Buurtverschraling,

Scheld'apen, nodigen u hierbij uit aanwezig te zijn op de inhuldiging van «'t Pand» als Beschermd Monument.

AANKONDIGING
OFFICIELE INHULDIGING
BESCHERMD MONUMENT
SCHELD'APEN - 't PAND
d'Herbouvillekaai 36
2020 Antwerpen

gekadastreerd AFD 9 – sectie I – 2797a/2

Lot 1. 19u Receptie

Lot 2. 20u Officiële Inhuldiging

Lot 3. 21u Start Feestelijkheden

Met muzikale omlijsting door: Robedoor, Team Panini, Sickboy, Nieuwzwart Trio, De Heer Tyfus, Sand Circles, Dynasty, Floris Van Hoof, Daniël de Botanicus, Gerard Herman en Ontzaglijk Veel Meer...

ENIGE ZITDAG 12 Oktober 2013
Avondkledij verplicht!

«Zetwerk: Afreux, druk: Polyprint»

From the Photocopier to the Letterpress: Scheld'Apen through Print
Pia Jacques

Souvenirs of Scheld'Apen are still vivid ten years after its end. In this text, I propose to approach Scheld'Apen through a different angle: its collection of prints. The material assembled in this book and the information available on the former website of Scheld'Apen, which is still active, were the main resources. I'll be focussing on the designs of a small selection of works and take a closer look at the different printing techniques that were used. Each technique has their specificities, print run capacity, and cultural references, offering an insight into Scheld'Apen's evolution through its fifteen years of existence.

Today, the archive of Scheld'Apen's printed matter takes the form of a book, under the auspices of Benny Van den Meulengracht-Vrancx and Bent Vande Sompele. Yet the printed matter had a dedicated space in the former building. The posters of the different events which occurred throughout the years, covered the walls of the restrooms. Some editions were printed in such small amounts that the only copy left was found on those walls.

Scheld'Apen's archive has a rich diversity of makers: visual artists, graphic designers, musicians, and enthusiasts. They worked on a voluntary basis, at least until 2008[1]. Scheld'Apen presented itself as a 'free and experimental space in a city where there wasn't any'. The flyers, posters, and other printed material are for the most unsigned. The richness of Scheld'Apen came from the co-existence of different ways of working. The one organising a specific event at Scheld'Apen could also be the one designing its visual identity.

References to punk and underground culture in the first years of Scheld'Apen were important. The punk movement introduced anti-design as the refusal of professionalism and rejection of norms[2]. The dates on the prints refer to the day and time, rarely to the year of the event. This omission demonstrates a sense of urgency. The making process of the posters is often visible, that the viewer experiences as spontaneous, authentic, and alternative.

Scheld'Apen's First Poster: Squatting and DIY Culture

Scheld'Apen developed its own strategies of belonging, presenting itself as a welcoming space for non-conformity and experimental practices. Those who felt alienated from the conventions of society created a space of their own. The squatting movement often goes together with a 'do-it-yourself' mentality. Scheld'Apen followed this logic, making use of (re)appropriation strategies and spontaneous language.

The first graphic work (varia 12) drawn on a simple A4 sheet of paper, paved the way for the future identity of Scheld'Apen. A handwritten text informs about a meeting on squatting. Two cartoon figures accompany the text, resembling the Belgian cartoon characters 'Suske and Wiske'. They reoccur in the following communications of Scheld'Apen and introduce other characters in the same comic style with scars and punk haircuts. They are often shown vomiting, drinking, killing or cutting themselves, as well as dancing. Their behaviours show the non-conformity welcomed at Scheld'Apen.

In the first years, the graphic language of Scheld'Apen used a shock tactic. Their intentions were to offend, provoke and draw attention. The name 'Scheld'Apen' refers to the river Scheldt, which lays adjacent to the squatted building, and at the same time translates as 'swearing monkeys'. The visual language was explicit and violent, based on the appropriation of symbols. Its imagery came from childhood, obscenity, and mass media. It shared an affinity with anti-fascism and anarchy[3]. The taking-over of images was in line with the squatting ideology. This practice allowed imagining another vision within a normative structure, proposing a counterculture to the mainstream.

Scheld'Apen's language evolved through the years but continued using the same tactics for visual impact. The use of collage, handwriting, drawings, intentional spelling mistakes, and cartoons was abundant. The graphic language reminds the one of resistance, present in many subcultures across Western Europe[4].

Spontaneous Printing: The Photocopier as a Tool

Speed and direct access to the means of production were essential in the first years of Scheld'Apen, making the photocopier one of their favourite tools. Its versatility facilitated the integration of mass-media images. At the end of the nineties, the prints were mainly photocopied in black and white. The designers worked in the most direct way possible, for instance by only using black markers. Wobbly and thick frames create unity in the whole image. The background sometimes shows a skyline of high buildings referring to Antwerp's city centre.

The mass-media images were selected for their shocking effect or their potentiality of diversion such as normative representations of society, the nuclear family, and the bourgeois couple. Another theme is the depiction of control and symbolic animals such as gorillas or sheep. Scheld'Apen assembled images and texts through cutting and pasting. This technique was already present in punk and post-punk youth cultures in the mid-seventies. Known for its efficiency, unique works were created with a low financial investment.

Scheld'Apen incorporated symbols within existing images to create a new narration. The Swastika as a critique of fascism, the anarchist symbol, and the international squatting movement symbol are frequently used. Adding comic bubbles was also a way of making the images their own. They played with the absurdities of society, taking a humorous or critical turn in particular images.

For a poster designed in 2000, we can compare the original creation (2000 03 25 P) and the final photocopied result. The initial composition shows the different layers gathered together for the final design. At the top of the poster, the designer cut out letters selected from various sources to form the word SABOTAGE. Some of the letters were already photocopies. Music styles in different typographies and letterings surround the words BIG PARTY, outlined with a black marker and pencil. Underneath, the line-up of DJs is enveloped in a pencil-drawn background, reminding of the stroboscopic lights of the club. The lettering is created using different contrasts, demonstrating knowledge of the photocopier's effects.

Playing with Conventions: The Stamp

The re-appropriation of visuals was also realised by imitating the layout. Scheld'Apen's infiltrated the existing structures of society with visual tricks. One example is a party invitation designed as the Belgian train ticket. (2001 02 24 P). In the center of the invitation, the information is stamped on a white background and pasted on a dotted raster.

Public administrations use stamps for legal documents and certificates. The adoption of this tool was consistent with Scheld'Apen's spontaneity. This easy, quick, and hands-on printing technique allowed for the rapid production of promotional material. The paper was repurposed from left-outs gathered at printing shops. Consequently, every print had a different size. The organisers of the event distributed these to a selection of people they met at parties, based on their affinities and looks. (2001 08 25 F, 2001 10 13 F, 2002 03 02 F, 2002 05 25 F, 2001 04 14 F, 2001 07 14 F, 2001 02 24 F, 2001 04 14 P, 2001 07 14 F, 2001 08 25 F, etc.).

The stamps were composed by hand with prefabricated rubber letters. For a grunge look, the uppercase and lowercase letters were mixed up. The date, location, and names of the DJs were stamped randomly on the paper. Rasters or cutting marks from the printing shops are sometimes still visible, which calls to mind the economic systems behind the organisation of the event.

Experimental Typography: Dry Transfer Letters

Dry transfer letters made their appearance in the early days of Scheld'Apen. Dry transfer letters were pre-printed letters on transfer sheets and available in different typefaces and font sizes. The letter was set on the design by rubbing it with the help of a stylus or a pen, requiring no water or solvent[5]. It was an easy way of having clean results without the help of a qualified printer. Non-designers were able to function as professionals. Their accessibility also encouraged experimenting with the letter forms in unique ways.

The poster 'The night of the musician' of 2001 (2001 11 23 F) was composed exclusively with dry transfer letters. The square format resembles a vinyl cover, appealing to the alternative music scene. The designer intentionally rubbed on and off the letters to create cracks. The composition in itself becomes a whole, forming one cohesive image. What was important was to grasp the atmosphere of the night. Yet, the readability had reached its limits for some. In the poster retrieved from the toilets, someone felt the need to intervene. By passing over the letters with a black marker, the forms become letters once again.

An Artistic Input: Silkscreen printing

In the 2000s, a variety of printing techniques appeared in Scheld'Apen's prints, such as screen printing. This printing technique is the process of transferring a stencil using a mesh screen and ink onto paper or another material. It is a versatile way of printing with vibrant colour results. First used in advertising during the 19th century[6], screen printing rapidly disseminated in other domains such as art and fashion. DIY culture has a preference for this method because of its accessibility. Screen printing requires few skills and its equipment is relatively cheap.

At Scheld'Apen, new members with artistic backgrounds took part in the making of the visuals. Screen printing made the prints more colourful and illustrative. Many events from 2003 were collaborative, bringing new inputs. Scheld'Apen worked with organisations such as Rotkop, an independent and alternative artist's magazine; KRAAK, a nomadic organisation supporting experimental and DIY music, and Freaks End Future, a record store specialised in underground music. Together, they organised events such as magazine launches, concerts, and festivals.

The sense of spontaneity present in the first years of Scheld'Apen persisted in the drawings and letterings. Doodles, sketches, scribbles, cartoonish creatures, and crossed-out elements invaded Scheld'Apen's visual language. The use of bright colours makes the general tone lighter. Scheld'Apen imagery became disruptive with a more playful tone, like the party of dancing phalluses on the flyers of the Rotkop party of 2004 (2004 06 19 F).

The Digital Aesthetic: The Computer as a Design Tool

The computer had an important impact on the prints from 2003 onwards. This tool brought new imagery in the multiple identities of Scheld'Apen. The flyer of DEATH PATROL from 2004 was made by combining different computer programs.

The line-up is in a grid structure, created with a spreadsheet program. The surrounding digital doodles were made with a graphic editing program such as Paint, using different pen thicknesses.

In 2005, the flyers for a music festival (2005 06 25 F) remind us of the Ray Gun magazines art-directed by David Carson in the nineties[7]. The typography interchanges from black and white placed on a mirrored image of a dog or a white rabbit. Two typographies were combined: one is a block display typeface set in all-caps and the second is handwritten, made with a small and thick marker. The crossed-out mistakes and circled numbers give a spontaneous touch looking like someone drew on the flyer.

David Carson's style marked the grunge aesthetic and influenced designers around the world. He experimented in unique ways with typography, texture, and layering. The uprise of the computer played an important role in the diffusion of the 'Carson' style. Known for being very distinctive in appearance, how it looked was more important than readability.

The computer freed from certain constraints, as the flyers by Yannick Val Gesto testify. (2010 02 04 F). The pictures are sometimes pixelated, making their digital source visible. Photo editing programs influenced the visuals by altering the colours, adding gradients, and creating photomontages. The imagery is extracted from popular TV shows such as the Power Rangers, Goldorak, and children's toys. The careless handwriting evokes the idea of draft sheets with splashes of ink, crossed-out mistakes, and extra scribbles.

A Larger Scope: Offset printing

In 2005, the first program booklets made their appearance. Next to these, events still had their own posters and flyers. The material is progressively more and more printed with offset. Offset printing is one of the most common printing techniques used today for high quality and large quantities. This technique works with an inked image on a printing plate, which is printed on a rubber cylinder and then transferred to paper[8]. It is a highly technical process executed by professional printing companies.

This transition to offset printing is an important step. A wider public also required a bigger print run. The printing had to be externalised to qualified printers where the designers had less control on the production process. Scheld'Apen took a professional turn once they were recognised by the city of Antwerp as a youth centre. Certain responsibilities came with this acknowledgment such as maintaining a program, and communicating it in the best way possible. Legibility became more important for the communication of Scheld'Apen.

One of the first program booklets printed with offset is from 2007 and is a good example of Scheld'Apen imagery meeting larger print-run production techniques. It was printed in green and black on newspaper and folded in four. The images come from mass-media and advertising presenting a nuclear family, smiling faces, a bodybuilder, a complete pan set, and office chairs, among other things. This selection recalls Scheld'Apen's beginnings, questioning the normative codes of society. The typography combines different typefaces. The title 'lente Scheld'Apen' is written with cut-out letters from magazines, the program is aligned to the left in a serif typeface, the rigid structure of the text breaks throughout the page and dry transfer letters, composed in a punk-ish style, are used for the date of the events.

The Final Letterpress Printed Poster: The Establishment of a Monument

The last poster is an exception to the rule in the entire archive of Scheld'Apen's printed material, concluding their existence beautifully. (2013 10 12 P). The poster is the only one from the whole archive printed by letterpress, the oldest of the traditional printing techniques. In this technique, copies of an image or a text are reproduced by direct impression of an inked surface against the paper[9]. The text is, in this case, composed by hand using individual metallic and wooden types. Graphic designer Afreux, who also made other works for Scheld'Apen, realised the letterpress composition at the Polyprint company.

The appropriation of graphic references from the public realm is one of Scheld'Apen famous tricks. When the city of Antwerp establishes a new monument, the information about the official inauguration is printed in a poster format with black type and yellow paper. The closing of Scheld'Apen presented itself as the inauguration of a protected monument. The poster imitated the city's official communication. Scheld'Apen organised a reception, festivities, and a gift shop. You could buy souvenirs such as maquettes of the building. Beers, spoons, and mugs on which a picture of Scheld'Apen was printed were also available[10]. The official sign 'beschermd monument' was nailed on the building that evening. In the Scheld'Apen spirit, the final event played with the conventions of authority.

[1] 'Over Scheld'apen', Scheld'apen, consulted on the 15.03.2023, http://www.scheldapen.be/?action=about&sub=437
[2] Paul Guerra and Pedro Quintela, Punk, Fanzines and DIY Cultures in a Global World: Fast, Furious and Xerox (Cham: Springer Nature Switzerland, 2020), pp. 5-6, https://doi.org/10.1007/978-3-030-28876-1
[3] Ibid.
[4] Ibid.
[5] Tom Vinelott, 'How to Apply Letraset Dry Rub-Down Transfers', Action-Transfers, consulted on the 18.03.2023 https://www.action-transfers.com/html/a_articles/what7.shtml
[6] 'What is Screen Printing?: How it works, Benefits & Applications', consulted on the 20.03.2023, https://www.ynvisible.com/news-inspiration/what-is-screen-printing
[7] Edd Norval, 'David Carson - The Messy Type', Compulsive Contents, consulted on the 18.03.2023, https://www.compulsivecontents.com/detail-event/david-carson-the-messy-type/
[8] 'Offset Printing', Britannica, consulted on the 20.03.2023, https://www.britannica.com/technology/offset-printing
[9] 'Letterpress Printing', Britannica, consulted on the 20.03.2023, https://www.britannica.com/technology/letterpress-printing
[10] 'Laatste Eindfeest', Scheld'apen, consulted on the 20.03.2023, http://www.scheldapen.be/?action=media&albumid=2653

Scheld'Apen Calendar (1998-2013) and Image Index

1998

06
- 18-19 Squatted
- 23 Volxkeuken
- 25 Kampvuur en A'peningsfeestje

07
- 01 Volxkeuken
- 02 Apeningsfeest (2): Con&Rot, Muggles, Insane Youth, LTS (FR), DJ Sloef.
- 03 Apeningsfeest (2): Kardiak, Honey Honey, Grover (UK).
- 04 Workshop Boomhutten
- 05 Workshop Percussie
- 07 Piratenfeestje in de tuin
- **08** Full Moon Party: Da Freakmothers, DJ Babba, De Walhala Flashers, Da Wiz-stix. **Flyer by unknown artist**
- 10 Volxkeuken
- 15 Occupada Nachta: Campain, Völkermord (DE), Hybernation (GR)
- 18 Workshop bierbrouwen + Volxkeuken
- 23 Occupada Fiesta: Re-Sisters (CH), Ebola (DE), Intestinal Disease (DE)
- 29 Not Yet, Quetzal, Scale Sheer Surface (US), Harriet The Spy (US)

08
- 02 Workshop automechanika + Volxkeuken
- 06 Volxkeuken: Vegetarische BBQ
- **09** Bashment '98: D'Penthouse, Overproof, Jah Shakespear, Back O'Wall, Bong Productions, Radical Dub, Fiji Sounds, Far West Crew, Back II Bass, Nyabinghi Sound, Bass Culture. **Flyer by unknown artist**
- 10 Antweurp Arrogance: Active Minds (UK), Third Degree (PL), Months of Birthday, Bad Influence
- 14 Anaal Kabaal: Mind (DE), Arsedestroyer (SW)
- 17 Stack (DE), Ebola (UK)
- **27** Stad Onder Stroom Deel 1: La Grande Bouffe. **Flyers by unknown artist**
- 29 Radio Underwhere presents Aire airlines goes Himalayas: DJs Pipco, Fiji
- **30** P.A.I.N (UK), Visions of War, Syc. **Flyer by Dennis Tyfus**

09
- 04 The Soundtrack of Your Suicide Festival: Mangenerated, Hellfiller, Waltrat, Hermit, Jalopaz + Workshop automekaniek.
- 07 Workshop jongleren, workshop jammen en vrije expressie muziek + Piratenfeestje in de tuin
- 12 Workshop fietsreparatie en SKA party: Looking Up, DJs Cindy, Martine, Bertrant
- **14** Workshop Teepees bouwen + Benefietconcerten ten voordele van dierenrechten: Sin Dios (ES), Insane Youth. **Flyer by unknown artist**
- **17** Alcatraz (FR), Liselotte (CH). **Flyers by Dennis Tyfus**
- **22** Doom, Rubbish Heap. **Flyers by Dennis Tyfus**
- 24 Rot (BRA), Abuso Sonoro (BRA), Entrails Massacre (DE) (probably rescheduled to 1998/10/01)

10
- **03** Nocturnal Emissions (UK), Deep (DE). **Flyers by Dennis Tyfus**
- **04** Sthraler 80 (AUS), Placebo, Seized (CA) + Workshop lassen en jongleren. **Flyer by Dennis Tyfus**
- **16** Sirke (LE), Sarkana's Oktobris (LE), Rayspeedway A.T. Devils of Space + Workshop percussie + Rave Goa DJs: Aorta, Gelflin, TMC Live, Techno DJs: Meniac Dynamic, Shamaan, SFÖ, Bacteriologic, Toxin, Maculae PH, Lunatic Live. **Flyer by Dennis Tyfus**
- 22 Kill Flavour (DE), Blendwerk (DE)
- 23 Workshop lassen + Chaos Feast feat. Heimatglück, Charlie Don't Surf, Jail Queer Burfers, DJs Marv Barv, Bootsie, Zotte Sof
- **31** Belgian Asociality, Freestyle Fabriek. **Flyer by Dennis Tyfus**

11
- 10 I Love The Smell Fest: Cornucopia, Ulrike's Dream, Midget (DE)
- 14 Shapes&Colors, Think of One + Marrakesh Emballage System (BE, MA)
- **20** Heimatglück (DE), 30.000 Kollegen (DE), Personenschaden (DE). **Flyers by unknown artist**

12
- 05 Reggae Jam: Overproof + Back 2 Bass + Far West + Bong Product
- 07 Jaded (DE), Stifled Cries
- 13 P.A.I.N (UK)
- 19 The O'Hara's, The Spanners
- 21 51 Days (UK), Eradicate (SCT), Confront Yourself
- 26 Deadzibel (AT), Valina (AT)
- 27 The O'Hara's Birthdayparty
- 31 Skankin & Slamming into 1999 + Jan's Birthday: Ska & Punk, DJs Gregor, Jan

1999

01
- 08 PCP (NL), La Fraction (FR), Infaust (DE)
- 26 Krzycz (PL), Hole Filler, Station Grey
- 30 Far West Crew

1999

02
- 06 — Open Air Birthdayparty
- 12 — Honey Honey + Not Yet B-dayparty
- 17 — Edna's Goldfish (US) + more, Ska!
- 20 — D'Rotzbauwen (LU), Petrograd (LU), Charlie Don't Surf

03
- 09 — P.A.I.N (UK)
- 13 — Far West Crew
- 19 — The Soundtrack of Your Suicide Part III: Rottenpiece (US), Recalcitrant (NL), FCKN BSTRDS (NL), The Faxxxed
- 23 — Jaded (IT), Vomit Fall (IT), Human Side (DK), One X More
- *28* — Debris (UK), Algonelgone Gnie (DE). ***Poster by Dennis Tyfus***

04
- 01 — Under The Gun (BE, SP, UK)
- 02 — Regga Régé Blast: Fuji + Overproof
- 07 — Code 13 (benefiet): Ebola (DE), Oi Polloi (SCT), Code 13 (US)
- 10 — Greece Hardcore Fest: Stateless in the Universe (GR), Free Yourself
- 17 — Aorta e.a., EX Cathedra, Counter Attack
- 23-24 — Pünxpicnic (Benefit voor Assata): Quetzal, Anaal Kabaal, René Binamé, LTS (FR), Not Yet, Senseless (HR), Link (FR), La Fraction (FR), Cluster Bomb Unit (DE), Heimatgluck (DE), 30.000 Kollegen, Apatridi (HR), Accion Militante, Assata, She Who Struggle, Women Talk & Action Group
- 30 — Grande Fiesta De La Familia Antifarez

05
- 03-10 — Fantastival (expo 99): Loterie Lokale, Shoeberg, Electric Fans, Feelburg Antidillus un Mechanism, Musica Bomba, Dizzy Brown, Think of One, Antifare, Brian The Scientist (NL), Mad Dog Olli & the Bones
- 07-09 — Fantastival (expo 99): Zounds, Aquated Waterbands (NL), El Guapo Stuntteam, Feelburg Stemkunstenares (NL), Living Tornados, Station Grey, Electric Fans, Wuynguns
- 12 — Syc, Revearsal of Man, Rubbish Heap
- 14 — Reggae Dance Pomdi Corner met Jah Shakespear
- 21 — Woofer Sound Lab met Flip Da Switch, Phineas, Jordy
- 24 — Rashid et Les Ratons (FR), The End of Ernie, Pluck, Shorty
- 26 — Citizen Fish (UK)
- 29 — The Legendary Soldiers: Murdock, Tinez, Raphaël

06
- 09 — HeaDJam (UK)
- 11 — Birthdayparty
- 16-18 — Eindejaarsvoorstelling Studio Herman Teirlinck: (Joi de Vivre)
- 19 — 1 Jaar Monkeybisnis: Piraten & Pipi Langkous feest
- 25 — Conspiracy Records Concerts

07
- 02-03 — Pünxpicnic (garden summahshit): .vuur., Seein' Red (NL), Ciderfex (UK), Hernandez (UK), Shank (UK), Baffdecks (DE), Klein Verzet, Boycot (NL), Chineapple Punx (UK), Distress, Betercore (NL), Point Offew
- 10 — Inner Terrestials (UK)
- 17 — 2106-187 AD Stereophonic Records: Murdock, Tinez, Raphaël vs Dago aka Anton Price, Nekro, Jakusi
- 20 — Reggae met Bong Productions
- 26 — Ananda (FR), Thoughts of Ionesco (US)

08
- 08 — Reggae met Fiji Sound
- 17 — Concerts
- 20 — New Sun Event: Sunscape, various artists (Drum n bass, Ambient Techno, Trance)
- 26 — Moscow Emballages Ensemble, Think of One, Da Russian Connexion
- 31 — P.A.I.N (UK)

09
- 04 — Drum n Bass Bash: Murdock, B-Major, Soi (feat. MC Ebony) + Bong Productions
- 17-19 — Antwerpen Zoemt Vegas, Les Baudouins, Morts, Rai Uno, Admiral Freebee, Murdoch, Izo, Doctor Nacho en Glitterpoep, Beangoose, Horse, Slingshot, Zombie Bird House, Les Clachards Civilisés, Los locos de Belgica, Salmonella Orchestra, Münchaussen, Bosz, Lysergic, Muffin, SFO, Toxin Maculae, Cyclone en Meat Beat, Free Project Jazzygroovyjam
- 23 — Homomilitia (PL), Wasted Land

10
- 03 — Unruh (US), Systral (DE), Knut (CH), Rubbish Heap, 100 years of Forgetting

11
- 07 — X-milk

12
- 17 — Dance The Ska: Tatort (NL, DE), Ragga afterparty met Bong Productions
- 22-23 — Millenium Chaos Circus: Catharsis (US), Stifled Cries (7inch release), Station Grey, Stack (DE), Hybris, Submerge (FR)

2
0
0
0

01
- 15 Reggae and Ragga Vibes: Bong productions
- 21 Tachyon, The Internationals
- 29 Electro and Drum n Bass: Raphaël, Murdock

02
- 05 Winter Break: Raphaël, Murdock, Tinez, A
- 12 Bootcamp Drumnbass party: B. Major, MC Ebony, Panzar + guest
- 26 Muziekmakerij: Dimitri Elektro

03
- 04 Reggae and Ragga Vibes: Bong productions
- 17 Pavo presents: Unite Against Society, 88Mate, Captain Crunch, Splifftones
- *25* Sabotage Big Party: DJs Gregor Terror, Sab Zen, MAd Mario, Zeus. **Poster by Monoskito & unknown artist**
- *26* Third Eye Tribe (CA). **Poster by unknown artist**
- 31 Scraper: Ed&Kim, Raphaël, Murdock

04
- 13 Selassie I Soundcrew
- *15* KI Promotions & Gamorahsound proudly presents Bootcamp 2: Gamorahsound, B Major, MC Ebony, Panzar. **Poster by unknown artist**
- *21* Okotta, Jesus Cröst, Visions of War + Goa Party. **Poster by Tim Leten**
- 30 Cirq Fix: Naft, Antifare La Familia, El Guapo Stuntteam, Rad van Fortuin, Vitalski Talks, Lady Angelina, Maskesmachine, Les Tigresses

05
- 03 Stratford Mercenaries (UK) feat Steve Ignorant (Crass) & members of DOOM & DIRT, Uncurbed (SE)
- 06 Sabotage Big Party 2: DJs Mario Jr., Zen san, Gregor Terror, Zeus
- *11* Bassdrum Jr., DJ Marie Antoinette. **Poster by unknown artist**
- 15 Fiskales adhoc (CL), Sharpville (FI)
- 30 Minx Girl (UK), Spacecactus, Station Grey, Raphaël, Anton Price, Jane Shag Shop

06
- *02* Vettig Patje Presenteert: Quetzal, Rectify (UK), Bad Taste (ES). **Poster by Herwin Dewinter, Vettig Patje & Iggy Blauwers**
- 11 Party Time (Reggae Open Air): Dr Leonine, D-Style, Flash it up, Live: Batucada
- 13 Misfits of Ska: Mu 330 (US), Link 80 (US), The Chinkees (US)
- 17 Piraten en Pipi Langkous feest: 2 jaar Scheld'Apen + Vettig Patje Presenteert: P.A.I.N (UK), Scale Sheer Surface, Anitfare Live
- 22 Vettig Patje Presenteert: Varukers (UK), Fleas n' Lice (NL)
- *24* Cluster Bomb Unit, Skew Wiff, Katastrophobia, Volkermord, Nahenoe Vernichtung, Detritus. **Poster by unknown artist**
- *29* Illectro Drumnbass: Raphaël, Murdock, Tinez, A. **Flyer by Tom Tosseyn**

07
- 01 AJC Scheldapen presents: The Internationals, Unite Against Society, The Pleeboys, The Jesters, Casualties
- 09 Vettig Patje Presenteert: Citizen Fish (UK) & Tachyon
- 14 14 Juillet Pierre Elitair
- *16* Summer In The City: Scheld'Apen Sunday's Project. **Poster by unknown artist**
- 18 Ananda (FR), Shora (CH), Inane (DE), Vuur
- 19 Abstain (US), 8 Days of Nothing (SE), Comrades (IT), Trapdoorfuckinexit (SE)
- *27* DSR Lines. **Poster by DSR Lines**
- 29 DOZER presents Illectro vs Drum n Bass: Murdock, Miyu, Raphaël, Tinez, A, Soi, Mentor, Ricky-D, Lupa

08
- 02 Lowlands & Stereophonic Records: Diskono (UK), Docktor Barnes (Diskono DJ), Advocaat, Alejandra & Underwood (US), DJ Hank, Raphaël, Lucky Kitchen
- 03 Bar Celona + Volxkeuken
- 05 PsychoAmbiElectRock: DJ Dolby Surrender (DE), Bassdrum JR, Susan Screentest (DE), Urlaub in Poland (DE), DJ TomH
- 09 Peaceful HC/Punk Event: Head Up, SL-27, Bob's Bizarre Bazaar
- 10 Bar Celona + Volxkeuken
- *13* Brazen (CH), Switchblade (SE), Winston (DE). **Poster by Janus 'Prutpuss' Lemaire**
- *17* Reggae Ska! Hiphop: 88Mate, Sint Andries Mc's, Freestyle Fabriek, Far West Crew, Internationals, Antifare, Scale, Tachyon, Zen. **Poster by unknown artist**
- 21-31 Toneel: Verknaarde - Joi de Vivre
- 22 Leia, Children of Fall, Exit 19
- *24* Disco Flash Dance Night (Disco in Bar Celona): DJ Meester X, Discobar Discordia. **Flyer by Dennis Tyfus**
- 31 Bar Celona + Volxkeuken

09
- 02 Submission Hold (CA), Petrograd (LUX), Voorhees (UK), Not Yet
- 06 Jeniger (DE)
- 07 8-koppig verjaardagsfeest van vrienden uit de Monty
- *11* Vettig Patje Presenteert: Sick on the bus (UK), Not Impressed. **Poster by Herwin Dewinter, Vettig Patje & Iggy Blauwers + unknown artist**
- *16* Vettig Patje Presenteert: Bad Influence, NotYet, DJs Denis, Rukkende Roger, Discobar Discordia, Robbie Robberechts, Pat Stevens + Bar Celona + Volxkeuken. **Poster by Herwin Dewinter, Vettig Patje & Iggy Blauwers**
- 23 Bloodcold (US), Happy Spastics (SCT), Between The Lines + Bar Celona + DRUM 'N BASS: Dice, Brekit, Murdock, Soi

2000

09
- 28 Bar Celona + Volxkeuken
- 29 Tarrantism (UK), Unite Against Society

10
- 14 The Heartaches, Foxy (US)
- 23 Guyana Punchline (US)

11
- 04 DJ Zeus, Terror
- 10 Forward to Zion bash: Fiji Sound feat. Captain Kirk, Crucial Alphonso
- 11 Vettig Patje Presenteert: iT! (UK) with conflict drummer Paco, No Reason Why.
- 15 Acid Mothers Temple (JA), As Ursin, Yenovak (RU), Frequency LSD
- 23 Macht van de Nuzikant: Punkistan, D.A.A.U., Think of One
- *25* Gilles' birthday PARTY: heksen & vampieren feest, El Chaupo Stuntteam + Antifare. ***Poster by Roos Janssens***
- 27 Valina, Salmonella Orchestra

12
- 01 DoZer: A, Raphaël, Tinez, Murdock
- 06 Hrvatski (US), Raphaël, Anton Price
- 08 Lecho (Sunscape) presents What-U-Waitin 4
- 16 Akira (DE), Insult (NL), Vuur
- *22* X-mas Time a Come: Winniemand Sound (NL), Far West Crew, Civalizee Foundation, Highgrade Soundclash. ***Poster by unknown artist***
- 27 Catacombo, DJ Le Grand Cristian
- 28 Rocket n°9 Take Off

2001

01
- 04 Volkskeuken
- 06 Vettig Patje Presenteert: AK 47 (HR), La Kurtizana (HR)
- 06 Nezavisni Teatar, Barake
- 11 Volkskeuken
- 18 Volkskeuken
- *19* Verboden Amoeder mee te brengen fuif: Door & Voor Chiro Dolfijn. ***Poster by unknown artist***
- *21* Vettig Patje Presenteert: Less (UK), Scale Sheer Surface, Detritus. ***Poster by Herwin Dewinter, Vettig Patje & Iggy Blauwers***
- 25 Volkskeuken + Dartstoernooi
- 27 Fête au Village: 88 Mate, Mystic Percussion

02
- 01 Film: The Matrix + Volxkeuken. ***Poster by unknown artist***
- 08 Film: Once Upon a Time in The West + Volxkeuken
- 10 Dynamite Pilot, Ernst H. Störznender: Oude, nieuwe golf
- *15* Radio Centraal Presenteert: Italian Freejazz: Carlo Actis Dato, Enzo Rocco, DJ Snaporaz + Volxkeuken. ***Poster by Dennis Tyfus***
- 22 Film: Anatopia + Volxkeuken
- *24* Electro #1: Steffi, Steven De Peven (NL), Raphaël, Anton Price, Stijn. ***Flyers & Poster by Raphaël Vandeputte***

03
- 01 Volxkeuken + DJ Zen
- 03 Far West Crew, Crucial P., Boombastic Soundsystems
- 08 Volxkeuken + DJ Alfred
- 15 Guapo (UK) + Volxkeuken
- *17* Bulbul, Blutch. ***Flyer by Nick van den Hurck, printed by Janus 'Prutpuss' Lemaire***
- 22 Volxkeuken
- *24* DoZeR: Tinez, Raphaël, Murdock, A. ***Flyer by Tom Tosseyn***
- 29 Volxkeuken + Open Jam Podium
- *30* Mörser (DE), The Deadly Rhythm. ***Flyer by Janus 'Prutpuss' Lemaire. Poster by unknown artist + Conspiracy Records***
- *31* Shaddap You Face: DJ Zen + guest DJ. ***Poster by unknown artist***

04
- 05 Vettig Patje Presenteert: Shock Treatment (IT), Cast Down + Volxkeuken
- 07 Down by the River feat. High Grade Sound, Back 11 Bass, Crucial P
- 12 Toogconcert Pandartiesten + Volxkeuken
- *14* Electro #2: Raphaël, Stijn (Live), Goodwill, Foreign, Kid Goesting. ***Flyers by Raphaël Vandeputte***
- 19 Volxkeuken
- 25 Greg's B-Day Party
- 26 Volxkeuken
- 28 Full Lunatics Event: Sons of Sinatra, Pain, Discobar Discordia

2001

05
- 03 — Volxkeuken
- **04** — Bomboclaat Star !!!: Selassie I Soundsystem, Bong Productions Soundsystem. *Poster by unknown artist*
- **08** — Sunshine (CZ), Tripoli. *Flyer by Janus 'Prutpuss' Lemaire*
- 10 — Citizen Fish (UK) + Volxkeuken
- 15 — Fiskales Adhoc, Sharpville
- 17 — Dartstoernooi + Volkskeuken
- 19 — Toy Death (AU) + Dozer: Illectro/Drumnbass Mash Up: Tinez, Raphaël, Murdock, A
- **24-25** — St. Cecilia's Cirq Fix: Think of One, 80 jarige Tapdansers, Maskesmachine en de Gasten, Lady Angelina, Ateliers De Makerij, Dharmische Dierenfopperij, Toy Death + Volxkeuken. *Flyer by Dennis Tyfus & Kevin 'Apetown' Van Gaver*
- 31 — Volxkeuken
- 31-... — Fantastival 2: Petrol Stelt Tentoon

06
- ...-03 — Fantastival 2: Petrol Stelt Tentoon
- 07 — Volxkeuken Open Air
- 14 — Volxkeuken Open Air
- 16 — 3 Jaar Scheld'Apen Superheldenfeest verschillende gastoptredens en DJs
- 21 — Volxkeuken
- 23 — Party Time Again (Open Air Happening): Cindrella, D Style, Flash it up. *Poster by unknown artist*
- **28** — Conspiracy Records Presents: Tarentel (US) + Volxkeuken. *Poster by unknown artist + Conspiracy Records*

07
- 05 — Volxkeuken Open Air
- 07 — Erik's Boerenfuif
- 10 — Unity Gig Part 2: The Spanners, The Agitators, The Internationals, DJungle Foufou, Banteon Rococo, Fiji Sound
- 12 — Volxkeuken
- **14** — Electro #3: Stijn & Raphaël, Spacid. *Flyers by Raphaël Vandeputte*
- 18 — The Black Heart Procession (US), El Torturado
- 19 — Volxkeuken BBQ
- 23 — Driven (NL), Broken Promises, Burn Hollywood Burn (FR), One Truth (IT), DJ Joe Ventura, Humorous Suprise acts
- 26 — Volxkeuken
- 28 — Drum'N'Bass: Dylan, Murdock, Shorty, Soi, hosted by MC Ricky D

08
- 02 — Volxkeuken
- 09 — Volxkeuken
- **16** — Eejties Disc Oh Flash: Pat Stevens (is jahrig), Robbie Robberechts, Ivonne van Gils + Volxkeuken. *Flyer by Dennis Tyfus & Kevin 'Apetown' Van Gaver*
- 23 — Volxkeuken
- **25** — Electro #4: Goodwill (Live), Raphaël, Stijn (Live), &...? *Flyers by Raphaël Vandeputte*
- 30 — Video Cirq Fix + Volxkeuken

09
- 06 — Volxkeuken + DJ 1S
- 13 — Volxkeuken + DJ DBXL
- 19 — Sekta core! (MEX)
- 20 — Volxkeuken + DJ Alfred
- **22** — Subdeviant Night: Llips, Bohrbug, Cassini Division, House of Low Culture (US). *Poster by Dennis Tyfus*
- 24 — The World/Inferno, Friendship Society (US), The Hobo Kings (Queer Cabaret F.)
- 27 — Volxkeuken

10
- 04 — Film: Spinal Tap + Volxkeuken
- 11 — Film: Barfly + Volxkeuken
- **13** — Electro #5: Raphaël, 2 Jeunes Hommes de Bruxelles. *Flyers by Raphaël Vandeputte*
- 18 — Film: Black Cat White Cat + Volxkeuken
- 25 — Volxkeuken
- 27 — Strandgitanefest: Kocani Orkestar (MA), Think of One met Naft, Magic Tiger (Kraakfanfare Brussel)

11
- 01 — Volxkeuken
- 04 — Pleasure Forever (US), The Fucking Champs (US), Hitch
- 08 — Volxkeuken
- 15 — Steve D. + Volxkeuken
- 17 — Drum'n'Bass Bash 5: Murdock, Wasp & Panzar, Blade Runnaz, Lium&Headz
- 22 — Volxkeuken
- **23** — Nacht van de Muzikant: De Bossen, jamsessies. *Flyer by Dennis Tyfus*
- 29 — Volxkeuken
- **30** — Eejties Disco Noebiet Flash Meeester X, Pat Stevens, Techniks Jan. *Flyer by Dennis Tyfus & Iwan Verhulst*

12
- 04 — As Friends Rust (US), Strike Anywhere (US), Thumbs Down

2001

12
- 06 — No Parasan 2: DJ Zen + too many shit DJs + Volxkeuken. *Flyer & Poster by Zen Declerq*
- 08 — Far West Crew
- 13 — Volxkeuken
- 20 — Volxkeuken
- 22 — DoZeR Illectro - DNB: Raphaël, Tinez, Murdock, A. *Flyers by Tom Tosseyn*
- 27 — Volxkeuken
- 31 — Oudejaarsavonddiner

2002

02
- 09 — DoZeR DRUM'N'BASH nr. 6: System-D (DE), Murdock, Woodcarver (NL)
- 15 — Disco Verkleed-in-wat-je-wil Party: Bredda, Simon, Thierry Tramblotte, Klecktic. *Poster by Saar Vangenechten*
- 22 — Worst Nationaal Paard 1: El Guapo Stuntteam, The Bones (NL), The Heartaches, Raphaël, videoprojecties

03
- 02 — Electro #6: Raphaël & Stijn. *Flyers by Raphaël Vandeputte*
- 08 — Intergalactic Funk: Jan Technics, Philip, Dago. *Flyer by primastyle.be*
- 20 — Conspiracy Records Presents: Trumans Water (US), I'm Being Good (UK)
- 30 — Log On To The Yardlink: Fiji Soundsystem, Red Alert Sound, Fella feat. Raggamuffin Whiteman, Sista G, Future D (JM)

04
- 06 — 1 Jaar 't Hemeltje: The Agitators, The Heartaches, Tachyon, 88Mate, Los Putas, Graveyard Slut, Hardsell. *Poster by Tom von Lucky*
- 13 — DoZeR, Illectro Digger Bucket Assembly: Raphaël, Tinez, A
- 21 — Conspiracy Records Presents: Sunshine (CZ), Quetzal, White Circle Crime Club. *Flyers by Nick van den Hurck. Poster by unknown artist + Conspiracy Records*
- 27 — Stereophonic: Robo & Audiobot Release Party: Thee Vaporizer, Sickboy, Stroheim, Raphaël, Slammer, Senjan vs Died. *Poster by unknown artist*

05
- 04 — DoZeR D'N'BASH nr. 7: Dylano, Pan, Murdock, Working Crash Hero. *Flyer by Tom Tosseyn*
- 08 — Conspiracy Records Presents: Electric Wizard (UK), The Plague of Gentlemen
- 10 — Drum 'n Bass Manga: Morphineas, Tiger, Breezer, Nag, Flip da Switch
- 17 — Conspiracy Records Presents: 90 Day Men (US), Vandal X. *Flyer by Nick van den Hurck*
- 25 — Electro #7: Stijn & Raphaël. *Flyers by Raphaël Vandeputte*
- 30 — Conspiracy Records Presents: Arab on Radar (US), Kid Commando (SE), Jockary. *Flyer by Dennis Tyfus. Poster by unknown artist + Conspiracy Records*

06
- 15 — 4 jaar 't pand: El Guapo Stuntteam, Discobar Discordia, DJ Delpierro. *Flyer by John Rausenberger & StephanBXL*
- 22 — BOO! (SA), Zaïus, Gigi Amaroso, Funky Fred, Steamy Fen
- 29 — Trutnultwee: Tintenkiller, Triskel, Rose Turteler, Shoowapps, The Riplets, Thaiti Twins, Ken Iris & Laura Garnier, Lady Jane, Steffi Klakson, Kika's Kitchen. *Poster by unknown artist*

07
- 12-19 — Petrol Zuid Pakt Uit. *Poster by Kevin 'Apetown' Van Gaver & Dennis Tyfus*
- 12 — Megahappening: Expo Opendeurdag, Iedereen Graaf Met: Papy het Paert, Jockary, Fuckoffdogs, Traktor, Think of One, La Familia, Mc Benny, Double Trouble
- 13 — Strandgitanefest: Ambrassband, Paleisfanfare, DJ Le Grand Christian
- 14 — BBQ-Picknick: Benjamin Verdonck speelt 313, Les Fanfoireux, Beversluisfanfare
- 15 — Pottoe (Efkes Nix)
- 16 — Megahappening: Expo, Opendeurdag, Filmchill, Luxe Volxkeuken
- 17 — Brientje Vertelt Baa De Gilles Aan Den Toog: Antwerp Attitude, Tyfus & Kevin Johnson, Ideal Tower + A! De sprekende ezels kraken: The Complicators + Luxe Volxkeuken. *Flyer by unknown artist*
- 18 — Fluxfilm + Volxkeuken: Rose Turtlertler (AT), One Louder, Maskesmachine: De Video, Ateliers Demakerij
- 19 — Petrol Zuid Pakt Uit: Monguito, Stroheim & Tomislav, DJs H&C (Stereophonic)

08
- 03 — DoZeR D'N'BASH nr. 8: Nojzz, Wontime, Murdock, PXP Crew (NL). *Flyer by Tom Tosseyn*
- 10 — Terrors of the Jungle: Dago & Morphineas. *Poster by unknown artist*
- 24 — Kidz Party: Latzi Jones (straatcircus), Kinderdisco, Pannekoeken
- 31 — DoZeR Strike A Pose: Stijn (Live), Raphaël, Murdock, A, Tinez

09
- 07 — De Bossen, Hara Kiri, Kalashnikov
- 18 — Traktor presenteert: Pakava It (RU), Wawadadakwa. *Poster by Saar Van de Leest*
- 28 — Yardlink Event: Flash It Up Sound, SynexFiji Sound, Red Alert Sound, Frass International (Fella & Future D)

10
- 25 — Audiobot/Stereophonic Records Present: Space Hustlers: JRD, Sosven Tomislav, Stroheim, Jan Technics, Boy Tronik. *Flyer by unknown artist*

11
- 02 — The Hub (US), One Louder, DJ Butsenzeller
- 05 — Conspiracy Records Presents: Scissor Fight (US), Dukes of Nothing (US), Sex Animals (US)

2
0
0
2

11
- 10 — Verkleed als Tourist: Dr Dog, Joris Jan
- *23* — Nacht van de Muzikant: Allerlei lokale superheld(inn)en,
De Gill Z'n Keel Al Een Kwart Eeuw Droog Mega Mega Mega Party Aan Den Toog
Flyer by unknown artist

12
- 04 — P.A.I.N, Counterattack, The Usual Suspects
- 07 — Attack/Decay/Sustain/Release: Jozefaleksanderpedro, ynri, DSR Lines, (Erzatz) & Halofaust
- *14* — Blast: Sickboy, Zero Tolerance, Scarecrow, Hysteresis. **Flyer by unknown artist**
- 20 — Valina (AT), My Ling

2
0
0
3

01
- 10 — Quetzal, Thunder Heart Machine
- 16 — Rose Turtlertler (AT), DJ Blauwers
- 25 — DoZeR Drum'n Bass/Electro: Murdock, Raphaël, Tinez

02
- 01 — Broekie's Beurtdee-Pwerty: Vibecraft, Detritus, Counter Attack, DJ Vettig Patje & DJ Boetsie1
- 07 — Allemaal Bijeen Of Ge Doe Ni Mee: The Fuckoffdogs, De Manne van Kaliber, DJs Peter Pipi & Jasper
- 14 — Starboner, Mescalina (PL)
- 22 — 25 Drummers!! Voor 25 jaar Boots op Drums en 35 jaar Boots op planeet

03
- 15 — Rotkoparty! Raphaël, Daniël en de Bling Bling Brothers, F44 video trash
- 22 — Electro #8: Raphaël + friends, Live Cosmic Force
- 28 — Electrolochmann (DE)

04
- 04 — Eddy Merckx Benefietfeesje: Bling Bling Brothers, DJ Tempeh & DJ Seitan, Sickboy
- 15 — The Curse of Zounds (UK), Newborn Neurotics
- 18 — The Hub: Avant Garde Jazz/Metal from Brooklyn NY: Captain Fistfuck and The Vulva's, DJs Unrestful & Butsenzeller
- 26 — Groot Kinderfeest

05
- 03 — 88Mate, Starboner feat. Mata Hari, Ow, Unleash The Fury, Mr Rotplaat, Eva1 + Eva2 = Stereo, Don Alfredo, Mighty Mouse
- 09 — Worst Nationaal Paard 2
- *17* — D 'N' Bash9: Leno, System-D, Pamb, Murdock, Mc Proskript, Mc Dart. **Flyer by Tom Tosseyn**
- 24 — Electro #8,5: Monkeyshop, L.eargoggle, Kassen, Orgue Electronique, Raphaël, TLR
- *29* — Babsley, Traktor Try Out met Hans Sax van Internationals. **Poster by unknown artist**

06
- 04 — Vettig Patje + Broekie presenteren: N.V.U., Harakiri, Mind Stab
- 14 — Rotator (FR), Electric Kettle (FR), Thee Vaporizer, Droon, Sickboy, T.Error, Bling Bling Brothers
- 28 — 5 Jaar Scheld'Apen op Sportkamp!: The Internationals, Donkey Punch, DJ Del Piero, DJ Tyfus & Daniël

07
- *05* — Rotkoparty #2: Raphaël, Sickboy, Tyfus und Daniël, Bling Bling Brothers, All night video trash. **Posters by Jelle Crama**
- *13* — Quatorze Juillet de Radio Centraal: DJ Pierre Elitair, DJ Maladie, DJ Daniël. **Poster by Kevin 'Apetown' Van Gaver**
- 18 — Noise!!!! Sonar, Ah Cama-Sotz, Hysteresis-Trimetrick, Dist.reality-Mc Fuzznut
- 25 — Opening Rotkop: A3 Xpo + Electro #9: Comtron, Rude66, Stijn, DJs Kid Goesting, Diepvries, Raphaël
- 26 — Electro #10: Cosmic Force, Hantrax feat. Liza, Stijn, DJs Il Disco, Tinez, Raphaël

08
- 14 — the Revolution: HVW8 (CA)+ Volxkeuken
- 15 — Schwartzwaldklinik, Raxinasky, DJs El Penguïno, Don Alfredo
- 16 — Air on Maiden, Newborn Neurotics, DJs Allesbrander, Superklit
- 17 — BBQ (Breng zelf eten mee) + Kortfilm tentoonstelling + Beversluisfanfare, Pakava It (RU) + Benjamin Verdonck
A-DSR Night: Ynri/DSR Lines, DJs Veinzer, Daft, Pietr
- 21 — Kidfest: Bootsie & Vincent, Latzi Jones + Motorama (IT), DJ Butsenzeller + Volxkeuken
- 22 — The Incredible Sucking Spongies, Scumlic, DJs Brienerschnitzel, Ginger
- 23 — The O'Hara's, Rarock Reset + DJs Tempeh, Magic Marker, Raxinasky, Schwartzwaltklinik

09
- 12 — Kontra Presenteert Audition (film van Miike Takashi), Stacks of Stamina (SE), Cavemen Speak,
The World After 4/02 (SE/BE), Kapp und Kutt Soundsystem, Bling Bling Brothers
- 20 — Conspiracy Records Presents: 27 (US), White Circle Crime Club, Mendez

11
- 01 — Flashdance Night Playback & soundmixshow, DJ Butsenzeller
- 07 — CD release party: Monolith, Hysteresis, Trimetrick, Distreality
- 22 — N/Macht van de Muzikant: Maskesmachine en tal van andere bekende muzikanten die van hun management niet op de affiche mogen staan van een gratis optreden

2003

12
- **06** De Ontmaskering van Sinterklaas: Banner, Chocotof, Raphaël. ***Poster by Monoskito + unknown artist***
- 13 Oops Wrong Planet! Rudy Trouvé Sextet, Spunk, Monguito
- 19 Benefiet-Feest Bukit Lawang Indonesia, DJs den oudste van De Vries en de lelijkste van Vermeylen

2004

01
- 24 Dutch Resistance: Infiltration: JRD, Lowani, Suy, Youri
- 31 Broekie's Birthday-Party: Raxinasky, 1 Louder

02
- 21 Rok Top 1 Year! Candie Hank (DE), Elvis Pummel (DE), Sickboy, The Lovechild Combo, Peet & De Teefjes (NL), Lulkoek (NL), Jada (NL), Crackremover & MC Cybershit (NL), Bling Bling Brothers, Daniël, Sultanz of Swing, Meeuw-Lap II top-DJ (NL).
- 28 Rawknight: Steamer Cry Wolf, The Hickey Underworld, DJs Peter, Jasper & zen rotplaten, Butsenzeller

03
- *20* Izostars, Autistic Youth, DJ Viking & friends+ Glenda's Panty Party. ***Flyer by unknown artist***

04
- 06 DoOoOM! Esoteric (UK), Udom, Pantheist, In Somnis
- 16 Chantal & Rachel Verjaren Verkleedfeest: DJs Butsenzeller, Crash&Burn, Jasper & zen rotplaten
- 17 DoZeR Brazil Benefiet: Murdock & Bambu
- 22 Conspiracy Records Presents: In-kata, Bulbul (AT)

05
- 07 Rotkop and (K-RAA-K)3 Present: Jason Kahn (US), Chimuser, The Soft Cushions = Dirk Freenoise, Mik Prims, Sultanz of Swing, (k.raa.k) non sound, Tyfus & Daanijel
- 13 Laaif Optredens Buiten: Schidzoid, A Kollen, Locklust, The Soft Cushions, Endless, Sgimuser + Volxkeuken
  Paartie Heel De Nacht!!! Pedro Horemans - Sultarzans of Zwing
- 15 Bank Robbers Ball: Benefiet voor International Fooball Club An Sibhin: DJ Wally & Guy, DJ Sunhine & Undaria
- 18 Surprise Concert + Party

06
- *12* Freaksendfuture Festival: Avarus (FI), Tomutonttu (FI), Crank Sturgeon (US), Mauro Antonio Pawlowski, Af Ursin, (BE/FI), DJs Sultanzzovvzwwing, Tyfus & Daniël, Brieno. ***Flyer by Jelle Crama***
- *19* 6 Jaar Scheld'Apen Deel 1/3: Kinderfeest + BMX-Demolition + Time-Circus + Kontra Openluchtfilm: 'Afropunk: The Rock n Roll Nigger Experience' + Rotkoparty!/Most sexiest Rotkoparty ever! Switch Sonata, The Skills (NL), Maskesmachine, Jack The Rapper, Sickboy & Owleygirl (AT), DJs Meeuw (NL), Brieno & Daniël, Stroheim, Totenkopf brigade. ***Flyer by unknown artist. Flyer by Jelle Crama***
- 24 6 Jaar Scheld'Apen Deel 2/3: 313/Misschien wisten zij alles: Willy Thomas & Benjamin Verdonck
  Kontra Openluchtfilm: 'Space is the Place' + Traktor, Time-Circus, Benjamin Verdonck + Volxkeuken-BBQ
- 26 6 Jaar Scheld'Apen Deel 3/3: Kontra Openluchtfilm: 'Sons of Osiris'
  Big Ape Party: A.M.Brassband, Butsenzeller, Raphaël, Time-Circus

07 ***Program Booklet by Janus 'Prutpuss' Lemaire***
- 14 Jour de Fête Quatorze Juillet de Radio Centraal: Pierre Elitaire
- 29 Squeezablefuture + Volxkeuken
- 31 Hypnoskull, Immenent Starvation, Frames a Second, Dr. Demon, Hysteresis, Trimetrick, Distreality

08
- 05 DJ Faesho & DJ Matchbox + Volxkeuken
- *08* Death Petrol Brunch Air + BBQ Movies: Floris Vanhoof, Koen Boyden, Adrien, Danielle Lemaire, Nyx.lum. Expo: Plin Tub, Koenie's Workshop Mail, Thomas Bartosik. Concert: Daft, The paralells, Girl en lawaai, The Joyous Cosmology, Formatt, Der Draaiguitaar, Sickboy, Buffle, Saturn Dreams, Flash Bunny & Syncopated Elevators Electric Circus, R.O.T., Building Transmissions, Consultans, Benjamin Franklin, The Vegetable Man (In zijne auto!), Koenie's Workshop Speach, Anatole Tesla, Microhm, Patrick Thinsey, Mauro, Locklust, Fibercast Mold, Danbert, TBTTBC, Moysk vs. Kimujser, Thee Vaporizer, I Love Sarah, Schizoide, Christophe Albertijn, Vegas, Nico Rubeens, Maarten Tibos, Sonata Sines & Squares, Antistresspoweet, De Sfeermakerij, Ordinary Seaman, Marnix Tortelboom, Gart & Seekatze, 80000, Timik, Stefaan Quix & Thomas Olbrechts, 2/3 K 'Two Third of K', The Sift Cushions, Drifting Bears Collective, Huge Chinese, Spytrash. ***Flyer & Poster by Jelle Crama***
- 12 Laatste Volxkeuken: Noppes + Donkey Veggie
- 13 Deutschland — Volksmusik, Heimat und veel meer: DAF (DE/BE), Murena & Münch & Gabi Prinzip (DE), Ida Red (DE), Roxi Musik (DE)
- *19* La Fête des Allumeuses: OW + Happy Few, DJ Butsenzeller. ***Flyer by unknown artist***
- *27* The Jesters, 88Mate, The Agitators, Los Putas, DJ Zen & Terror. ***Flyer by unknown artist + Jol***

09
- *04* Eindfestival vd Huidige Locatie...: Maxon Blewitt, El Guapo Stuntteam, Kim Peers + Jorg Strecker, DJs Jonathan & Raphaël. ***Poster by Jonathan Jacobs***
- *05* Eindfestival vd Huidige Locatie...: In-Kata, Franco Saint de Bakker, The Internationals, Year Future, DJ Butsenzeller. ***Poster by Jonathan Jacobs***
- *28* Big Stream DiStrict Vs. Scheld'Apen Art Expo: Mudmen, Heartaches MC & DJ + Grafitti Jam + Opening Skatepark. ***Flyer by unknown artist***

2005

03
- **Program Booklet by ROTKOP & Kevin Van Gaver**
- 25 Openingsfeest! Monkey Business
- 26 Kontra Stelt Voor: De Letterleggers: Raphaël Vandeputte & Iwan Verhulst

04
- 01 Volxkeuken
- 02 Kontra Cinema: 'Themroc'
- 08 Volxkeuken
- 09 Kontra Cinema: 'Tierische Liebe'
- 15 Volxkeuken
- 16 Kontra Cinema: 'Mein Liebster Feind'
- 22 Volxkeuken
- 23 Kontra Cinema: 'Illegal Art'
- 29 Volxkeuken
- 30 Rothpetra: Nautical Almanac (US), Harry Merry (NL), Bloody Occurance (US), Surprise act van Gnarly DJ Team: Briener, Tyfoef, Crash and Burn, Matchbox Jean, Sharp & beast friendly projections

05
- 05 World/Inferno Friendship Society (US)
- 06 Volxkeuken
- 07 Kontra Cinema: 'Dial H-I-S-T-O-R-Y'
- 13 Volxkeuken
- 14 Kontra Cinema: 'The Corporation'
- 20 Volxkeuken
- *21* Kontra Cinema: Jan Svankmayer, The Brothers Quay + Animatiefilms. **Flyer by Kontra**
- *27* Death Petrol, Kraak and Ultra Eczema Present: The Ultra-Dead Buzzes of Heat Festival: Cerberus Shoal (US), Monopolka (RU), Mollenhauer, Cassis Cornuta + Volxkeuken. **Flyer by Dennis Tyfus & Kevin 'Apetown' Van Gaver**
- *28* Death Petrol, Kraak and Ultra Eczema Present: The Ultra-Dead Buzzes of Heat Festival: Smittekilde (expo, DK), Holiday Pills (DK), Butterknifekrush (DE), Buffle, Sickboy, Porkchoco & Yoko Brieno, DJs Dikzak, Lamzak, Platzak, Rotzak & Zeikzak + Volxkeuken. **Flyer by Dennis Tyfus & Kevin 'Apetown' Van Gaver**

06
- 03 Scheldapen Benefiet: Antwerp Gipsy Ska Orkestra, DJ Vincent, DJ Zen, DJ Gregor Terror + Volxkeuken
- 04 Kontra Cinema: 'The 5 Obstructions'
- 10 Volxkeuken
- 11 Kontra Cinema: 'Carlos' + Rothund + Tok Tek & Captain Peacock (NL), Bertin (NL)
- 17 Think of One Presents: 'Chuva em po' + Volxkeuken
- *18* Kontra Cinema: 'Hardcore' - Richard Kern. **Flyer by Kontra**
- *24* Scheld'Apen Festival (7 jaar Scheld'Apen): White Circle Crime Club, Franco Saint de Bakker, Creature with the Atom Brain, The Chinese Stars. **Flyers by Michèle Matyn**
- *25* Scheld'Apen Festival (7 jaar Scheld'Apen): Capsule, Music for Chickens by Robots, Benjamin Verdonck, Fugu and the Cosmic Mumu (AT), Tulip, die Singende Tulpe (DE), Thom Revolver (NL). **Flyers by Michèle Matyn**

07
- **Program Booklet by Janus 'Prutpuss' Lemaire**
- 08 Cindy & Martine Proudly Present: DJ Martine, Vini-Vici + Volxkeuken
- *09* Kontra Cinema: 'Haute Tension' + 'Rubber Johnny'. **Flyer by Kontra**
- *15* The Illektro Movement is Uppon Us Tekniks Jan, Stroheim, 3D Dance, 8-0-Freak. **Flyer by unknown artist**
- 16 Kontra Cinema: 'Repo Man'
- 23 Kontra Cinema: 'Barefoot Gen'
- 29 Schwarzwaldklinik + Volxkeuken
- 30 Kontra Cinema: 'Ne fait pas de Cinema'

08
- 02 Bulbul (AT), One Louder
- 03 Kontra Cinema
- 04 Kontra Cinema: 'Les Religions Sauvages'
- 05 Rotcrisistrotte Expo
- Duracell (FR)
- *06* Death Petrol No Luxe BBQ Festival: Permenant Death, Sudden Infant (CH), Elton Vincent, Elektrik Sonatas, Lawrence Wasser, Formatt, Bongoleros, Schizoide, Porkchoco, Orphan Fairytale, Antoine Chessex (CH), Tutto Fuzzi (D), Hondenkoekjesfabriek (NL), Ghost of Mercury, Masonic Youth (NL), Anatole Stretch, Picturesque, Norma X'Dout, Diskoster, Groote, Olivier Thys Groene Lul, Oms MNA, Speedy Trash Rock Band, Kobolten, SL-27, Black Hawai, Partdkolg, King Arthur and the knights of the round table, Syncopated Elevators Electric Circus, Curfew, Dirk Freenoise, Club Moral, Cassis Cornuta, LSD Mossel (NL), Hellfiller, Pentothal (F), Arsch Geil Redux (F), Lap!, Funeral Folkers, Ignatz, Surr Grr (F), Up with Piemel, mimes.lalie (F), Endiche (P), Laurent Impeduglia Infernal Stranbism Orchestra, Arentor Orchestra, Julian Bradley, Knust-extrapool, Antistrot (NL), Rotkop, Bram Borloo, Hondenkoekjesfabriek (NL), Kapreles, Le Dernier Cri (F), Strategie Alimentaire (F), Thilbault Delferiere (TBC), Smittekilde (DEN) **Flyer by Jelle Crama**
- 12 Undercurrent: Ynri, Mitsels, Picturesque, Creatures Like Us, Kiss the Anus of a Black Cat + Volxkeuken
- 19 Volxkeuken
- 26 Volxkeuken
- *27* DJ vs DJ Tigresse/Crash & Burn. **Poster by Annelies Van Opstal**

2005

09
- 08 Kontra Cinema: 'Aaltra'
- 09 Volxkeuken
- 10 Heartbreaktunes & Conspiracy Records Present: Asva (US) + Möse
- 15 Kontra Cinema: 'Strass'
- 16 Toooneeellleellel: Een lange avond met vijf korte solo's!: Simon Allemeersch, Nico Boon, Benjamin Verdonck, Abbatoir Fermé, Marijs Boulogne
- 17 Toooneeellleellel: Een na-zomer middag voor jong en ouder: Cie Bitskoem, Anna Vercammen en Joeri Cnapelinckx, Gert Dupont
- 22 Kontra Cinema: 'Where The Buffalo Roam'
- 23 Volxkeuken
- 29 Kontra Cinema: 'Moog'
- 30 Ultra Eczema & Freaks End Future Fest: Black Boned Angel, Syncopated Elevators Legacy, Ignatz

10
- 01 Ultra Eczema & Freaks End Future Fest: Jaap Blonk, Asra, Cassis Cornuta, Orphan Fairytale
- 06 Undercurrent: Barmitzvah Brothers (CA), The Two-minute Miracles (CA)
- 07 Volxkeuken
- 13 Kontra & La Fille D'O stellen voor: boekvoorstelling 'Lingerie & Lollypops' + Kontra Cinema Mashup
- 14 South American Assault: I Shot Cyrus, Migra Violenta (AR), Discarga (BR)
- 19 Hypnos, Los Natas
- 20 Kontra Cinema: 'Calvaire'
- 21 Volxkeuken
- 23 Broekie Presenteert: Raxinasky, Plastered, Hysteresis DJ
- 27 Kontra Cinema: 'Premanent Vacation'
- 28 Volxkeuken: DJ Marie
- 29 Undercurrent: Bluesanct Night: Drekka (US), Vollmar (US), Annelies Monseré (BE/NL)

11
- 03 Kontra Cinema: 'American Movie'
- 04 Volxkeuken: DJ Jonathan
- 10 Kontra Cinema: 'Dawn of the Dead'
- **11** Electro from Hell: Raphaël. ***Flyer by Jonathan Jacobs***
- 12 Soiree Yes, rejoice! You belong to the happy few: Enid Janssen
- 17 Kontra Cinema: 'Les Revenants'
- 18 Volxkeuken: DJ Veni Vici
- 19 Rotkoparty: Kunt (AUS), 2Chicks with Chainsaws, DJ Crash & Burn, DJ Carlo Audiorot, Body Of Aids
- 24 Kontra Cinema: 'Bukowski: Born into This'
- 25 Macht van de Nuzikant: Naft, Ambrassband, G's B-day Party, DJs Aku/Snof
- 30 Conspiracy Records Presents: The Psychic Paramount (US), tRAM

12
- 01 Ultra Eczema and Kontra presents, Tyfus Beurtdayparty: Hervatski (US), K.F. Whitman (US), J.M.H. Berckmans, Daniel, Dirk Ungawa
- 02 Volxkeuken
- 08 Kontra Cinema: 'Extension du Domaine de la Lutte', Houellebecq
- 09 Lo-An, DJ Butsenzeller + Volxkeuken
- **15** Kontra Cinema: 'The Wayward Cloud'. ***Flyer by Kontra***
- 16 Volxkeuken
- 18 Ultra Centraal: Felix Kubin (DE), DJ Daniël, DJ Bard Boetyrka

2006

01
- 20 Capsule, DJ Marie + Volxkeuken
- **02** ***Program Booklets by Janus 'Prutpuss' Lemaire***
- 03 Just Some Jazz Scum
- 14 Aids Wolf (CA)
- 23 Kontra Cinema: 'Ausländer Raus'
- 24 Heartbreaktunes: Deadstop/Seein'Red (NL), Career Suicide (CA), Fight Fight Fight (NL), Kantnochwal, DJ Aldolino

03
- 02 Kontra Cinema: 'Dumbland'
- 03 Le Club Des Chats (FR), Le Sport (FR), DJ Albanie, DJ Kania Tieffer
- 09 Kontra Cinema: 'Electric Dragon: 80.000 volts'
- 16 SLA-dag: Nico Rummens, Vitalski, Clitink, Haagse Witte, The Vags, Kuskearma Sopha, Tram, Believo, I Love Sarah, Schizoid, Seven, Laws of Who, Simple Songs, Pieter, Jelle, Hendrik, Arto, Bamboo, Lioness Redellation, United Steppaz, Sickboy, DJ Kutjong
- 24 Volxkeuken
- 31 Heaven Hotel Night: Teuk Henri, Tip Toe Topic, I Hate Camera, DJs: Elko B, Rudy T, Gunter N

2
0
0
6

04
- 05   31 Knots (US), I Love Sarah
- 07   In-Kata 'Farewell Masquerade' CD release: In-Kata, The Hickey Underworld
- 13   Kontra Cinema 'Haack'
- 14   Death Petrol: Magik Markers (US), Tuto Fuzzi (DE), Hans en Grietje, Shattered Minds, DJ Naughty Nathan, Diskoster, screenprints by Prutpuss & Crama
- 20   Kontra Cinema: 'Mzansi'
- 21   Some Girls (US), Malkovich (NL)
- 27   Kontra Cinema: 'I Know I'm Not Alone'

05   *Program Booklet by Janus 'Prutpuss' Lemaire*
- *05*   GoGoGo Airheart (US), Monno (DE). **Flyer by Dennis Tyfus**
- *11*   Ovo (I), Kania Tieffer, DJs Albani, Ju, Miss Belgium. **Poster by Janus 'Prutpuss' Lemaire**
- 12   The Hub (US) + Volxkeuken
- 18   Audio Eczema Nacht: Baby Dee (US), Panicsville (US), Viki (US), Magik is Kuntmaster (US), Kontra video trash slideshows, DJ Bart Botirka, DJ Tyfus
- 19   De Anale Fase, Kuskessarma
- 25   Kontra Presents: Roommate (US), DJ Dago (Anton Price)

06
- 02   Dry Speed, Batau Lavoir + Volxkeuken
- 04   Heavenhotel Presents: Franco Saint de Bakker, Papermouth
- *08*   Kontra Presents: Messer Chups (RU), Psychoacoustic Geographers (US), Guilty Connector (JP). **Flyer by Kontra**
- 09   Hitch, Thunder Heart Machine, DJ Butsenzeller + Volxkeuken
- *23*   8 Jaar Scheld'Apen!: Traktor, DJs Vini Vince, Daniël vs Snof. **Flyer by Janus 'Prutpuss' Lemaire**
- 30   Igor's B-day: The Disco Cybone, The Heartaches, DJ LC

07
- 08   Scheld'Apen Festival! i.s.m. Ultra Eczema: Jos Steen, Elvis Pummel, Amon Dude, Helicoptere Sanglante, Blood Stereo Ludo Mich, DJ Grow your own, DJ Daniël and Tyfus
- 28   Heaven Hotel Night: Shattered Minds, Borokov Borokov, Ow + DJs
- 30   Heartbreaktunes/Hypertension Records Presents Zombi (US), Hair Police (US), Fear Falls Burning, DJ Naughty Nathan + Brunch Time

08
- 04   Volxkeuken
- 06   Fait d'Anvers, Kuskessarma + Brunch Time
- 11   Anti-statique feestje! DJ Veni Vici + Volxkeuken
- 12   Death Petrol Presents: Ibiza Acoustica Festival Norma x'd out, Head of Wantastiquet (US/BE), Crank Sturgeon (US), Gastric Female Reflex (CA), Krokodillenland, Shattered Minds, Gart & Seekatze, Partkdolg, Penskyplochingen, art screenings, e★rock, Joeri Bruyninckx, Stratégie Alimentaire (FR), DJs Veg 18, Discobar Shorty, Bert Pels, Ultra Eczema, Audiobot, Veglia, Keen, Bread and Animals, Puik,...
- 18   Boekpresentatie: 'Polar Fury' Kika D. + Capital Scum, Ambrassband, DJ Kika D + presentation of Kika D's punk book + Volxkeuken
- 20   Kuskessarma + Brunch Time
- 25   Volxkeuken
- 26-27   Theater Braakland
- 27   Brunch Time

09
- 01   Dokter Ivago presente + Volxkeuken: Bart Maris, Les Poubelles, Whipped Tunes and Other Delight, Giovanni Barcella, Filip Wauters
- 02   DoorMouse (US), Sickboy, Droon, Beatlip, Hard-off (JPN), Sah se Lecter (NL)
- 03   Brunch Time
- 07   White Circle Crime Club (A Present Perfect CD/LP release party): White Circle Crime Club, Restless Youth (NL), DJ Afterfun: Matchbox Jef, Benny Tyfüsch, Roxi Popo, Peter Vdlintfabrique
- *10*   La Peau et Les Os (FR), Violenduo. **Flyer by unknown artist**
- *22*   Toooneeellleellel 2006: Skinsidout ★ Benjamin Vandewalle + Transmutation Device - Abattoir Fermé + Madame Fataal - Tuning People, Sunburned Hand of The Man (US), DJ Daniël 'N Briener. **Flyer by Dennis Tyfus.**
  Flyer & Program Booklet by ROTKOP & Kevin 'Apetown' Van Gaver
- 23   Toooneeellleellel 2006: Wewilllivestorm - Benjamin Verdonck + Warmhouwe - Ramona Verkerk + Monkey Business, DJ Marieke
- 27   Toooneeellleellel 2006: Warmhouwe - Ramona Verkerk + Buurman - Nico Boon, Tania Vandersanden, Dominque Van Malder + DJ Kid
- 28   Toooneeellleellel 2006: Kontra Presenteert: 'Please Love Austria!'+ On a March for Happiness March 1: Vienna Calling - Ernst Maréchal + Kontra Kortfilms + Film: Ausländer Raus (Schlingensief's Container) - Paul Poet (AT) + Valina (AT), DJ Crash 'n Burn
- 29   Toooneeellleellel 2006: Roadhouse Libra, DJ Croki Monsieur, DJ Moonchild + Volxkeuken
- 30   Toooneeellleellel 2006: Straattheatermarathon voor een Multiculturele Samenleving: Ben Zuddhist (UK), Abigail Collins (UK), Latzi Jones, David Cassel (CA), Theater Pili-Pili + Twee madammen, twee hoofden, twee tongen en nen hoop rommel - Janne Desmet en Kim Hertogs + De koffie staat op de tafel paard - Wanda Eyckerman, Peter Vandemeulebroecke + Grote hoop/berg, propositie 1: Reanimeren - Miet Warlop, DJ Houtsnip

2006

10
- 06   Toooneeellleellel 2006: Beatnacht + Kontra Cinema: 'I Was Born in Portland Town' + Think of One met Naft, DJs the Owl Jolsons
- 07   Toooneeellleellel 2006: 'Over naar jou' - Braakland/Zhebilding + Rfid-Ambassade: Rfid and Pervasive Computing - Rob Van Kranenburg (NL) + Thomas Smith and Alex Agnew, DJ Raphaël
- 08   Verkiezingsbrunch
- 10   Toooneeellleellel 2006: 'Dansen Drinken Betalen' - Braakland/Zhebilding + I H8 Camera, DJ Veni Vici
- 13   Toooneeellleellel 2006: Slotfeest: The Lieutenant of Inishmore - Olympique Dramatique + Guido Belcanto (in persoon), Kamerakino (DE), DJ Faster Pussycat
- 19   Ultra Eczema Knight: Lucky Dragons (US), Bobby Birdman (US), all night DJs and film loops
- **20**   Shora (CH). ***Flyer by Joachim Cols***
- **23**   Church of Misery (JAP), Sourvein (US). ***Flyer by Joachim Cols***
- 27   Well, Dada Swing (IT)

11
- **03**   Jean-Marie Berckmans' Eerste Psychotische Boekenbeursbal: Didi de Paris, The Chocolate Lovers, Peter Holvoet-Hanssen, De Vall, Bert Lezy, Shattered Minds, Jamez Dean Dabramski & Misses Dean, films van Wim Jamar, Seiben Kinder und ein Greis + Boekvoorstelling: Je kan geen twintig zijn op suikerheuvel: Jean-Marie Berckmans New Tirlemont Experience, Elvis Peters, Vitalski, Perverted by Desire. ***Flyer by unknown artist***
- **04**   Undercurrent #27: Noxagt (NO), Monno (DE), Penguins Know Why, DJ The Michael. ***Flyer by Undercurrent***
- 06   Ultra Eczema Knight: USA is a Monster (US), Animental (US)
- 09   Made Out of Babies (US), Black Cobra (US), Blutch
- 10   Paul Rose aka Scuba (UK), Dice, Goldorak, DLN, Karbonkid, G.O.T.C., Visuals by Teknar
- 18   Dutch Resistance (The Electro/Italo Edition): Alden Tyrell, Raphaël, Suy, JRD, Lowani
- 21   Sewer Election (SE), Bitter (NL), DJ Brain
- 25   Macht van de Nuzikant

12
- **08**   Blue Mountain Peaks: Crucial P., Zion Lions, Roots Bambu Sound. ***Flyer by unknown artist***
- 13   Ultra Eczema Knight: Chris Corsano, Paul Flaherty & Spencer Yeh (USA), Leslie Keffer (USA) + Danny Devos film loops, Jah Tyfus, DJ Daniël
- **15**   Tulip, Die Singende Tulpe (DE), Dead Western (US), DJs Tyfus, Naughty Nathan. ***Flyer by Jelle Crama***
- **16**   Poupi Whoopy Release Party: DJs Naughty Nathan, Sorry Sexpartners, Jack Feedback, Sickboy, Balbaard, acte de presence door Devilles Harem Girls + flirtatious projections. ***Flyer by Janus 'Prutpuss' Lemaire***
- 22   Nuit Blanche: DJ Crash 'n Burn, DJ Charlotte + laatste Volxkeuken
- **24**   Birthday Bash: Mariekes X-mas Mash: DJs Ungawa, Wart. ***Flyer by unknown artist***

2007

01
- 18   Gesloten ende Potdicht
- 19   Antwerp Gipsy-Ska Orkestra, DJ Butsenzeller + Volxkeuken
- 22   The Spores (US), DJ Aldolino
- 23   Vol project i.s.m. Belgat t.e.m. 8 februari
- 26   Volxkeuken
- 27   Kraak presents: Heathen Hearts Festival: Skullflower (UK), Marauder & Alibi (US), Anti-Ear (US), Silvester Anfang

02
- 02   Ultra Eczema Knight: Sublime Frequencies DJ Set (US), film: Sumatra Folk Cinema + Volkskeuken
- 03   Mokt Lawijt: Nag & Twan, Pt Kroe, Sput & CM, 2000WAT, Turbulent Flow Show, B-Man & DJ Brochette
- 08   Bar 219: Heartbreak Tunes Party: Angel City Outcasts (US), Enemy Rose, Old Smuglers, DJ El Penguino.
- **09**   K-Filmfest Presenteert The Kraken Awakens: Hysteresis live!, Sickboy, Droon, Vibro B, Dr. Sultan Aszazin, Beeld zonder naam, Amperror feat. Hantz, Partytrasher + Volkskeuken. ***Flyer by unknown artist***
- 16   Fuif SISO 2 Marco Polo Instituut: Volt
- 17   Ultra Eczema Night: Bill Nace (US), Peacemaker (US), Uske Orchestra, DJs Stroheim & Techniks Jan, filmloops van Lisa Jeannin
- 23   Wofo, The Blind Pilots Improvisers Orchestra, DJ Javiel + Volkskeuken

03
- 02   Lo-an, Ipah Straat Soundmachien & Toaster + Volkskeuken
- 08   Young James Long (US), Dyse (DE)
- 09   Scheld'Apen en Wood presenteren: Fathme Records on tour... Breakcore! Vytear (US), Eustachian (US), Sickboy, Droon, Beatlip, Dustrickx
- 16   Valsalva Rerun, Lasergoat, DJ Kid + Volxkeuken
- 17   Savage Republic (US), Creature with the Atom Brain, DJ Matchbox Jean
- 22   SLA-dag: Pieter Van Laer Big Band, Kuskessarma, Sopha, Alex Agnew, The Name of Hector, 1Tet feat. Cowboyjanetten, Valderama, DJ Steven & Wout, DJ Hendrik, DJ Pieter, Glenn
- 30   Mââk's Spirit (BE/FR), DJ Javiel

2007

04
- 06 — Heaven Hotel presents: Tip Toe Topic, Backback, DJs Bache J., Carlo A., Rudy T. + Volxkeuken
- 07 — Dutch Resistance invites Crème Organisation: Orgue Electronique (NL), Legowelt (NL), TLR, DJs Suy, JRD, Lowani
- 20 — Swimmers in Loch Ness, Thee, Stranded Horse + Volxkeuken Deluxe
- 27 — Untitled vs Bambu Present: Hijack (UK), Choolder, Kastor B2B Dice, Havoc B2B Karbonkid, DLN, United Steppaz, Quest Once MC (UK), Teknar

05
- 04 — The Go Find vs The Sedan Vault, DJ Croki vs DJ Faster Pussycat
- 05 — Van 't Straat Festival: De Bolwerkfanfare, Tupoley, Latzi Jones, Ad'eese, Juan Trunkyman, Circo d'ell Fuego, Lady Angelina, Ben Zuddhist, Kuskessarma, The Dump Brothers, Moustash
- *11* — Eat Rol: Yellow Swans (US), Onde, Laserquest, Blue Shift (US), Naomi, DJ Buffle + WWF: Save the planet + Volxkeuken. ***Posters by Jelle Crama***
- 16 — Stella Lanceert unieke marcellekes voor meisjes: DJs Wild at Aerts
- *18* — The Way of the Cross (US/FI), DJ Gross Glabelle + Volxkeuken. ***Posters by Jelle Crama***
- 19 — Cosmic Force (NL), DJ Raphaël, DJ Tomislav, DJ Stroheim, DJ Jan Techniks
- 24 — Theater t.e.m. 2 juni: Always Cry At Endings - Eisbär
- 25 — Made for Chickens by Robots (AU), The Mysterious Tapeman (NZ), Ow

06
- 09 — I Love Sarah, Self Service Nuts Club (FR), Bladder Gandhi (UK), DJs Elko B, Sjoerd B
- 15 — Blackie & The Oohoos Feest Clip: Stanton, Daddy's Darling, Violent Husbands, Blackie & The Oohoos + Volxkeuken
- 21 — Theater: Ziggy/Also known as 'Everybody knows this is nowhere, I'm really scared when I kill in my dreams' door Nicolas Delalieux
- *23* — 9 Jaar Scheld'Apen!!! FREAKS: El Guapo Stuntteam, Sickboy_Milkplus, DJ Kid, DJ Butsenzeller. ***Flyer by Janus 'Prutpuss' Lemaire***

07
- 02 — I.s.m. Heartbreak Tunes: Snöras (NO), Dominic (NO), Autumn Delay
- *07* — Ultra Eczema Presents: Viki (US), Extreme Animals (US), Stroheim vs H.A.N., video projections by Sunburned Taylor (US), DJs Daniël and special guest. ***Flyer by Dennis Tyfus & Kevin 'Apetown' Van Gaver***
- 14 — Radio Centraal's Quatorze Juillet: DJ Pierre Elitaire
- 16 — Ultra Eczema's Summer Bummer: Frying Membrane Boyz (US), Religious Knives (US), Anti Freedom (US/BE), Airport War (US), Damaged Goods, DJ Kak op Flik + BBQ
- 28 — Mauroworld.com presents: Mauro Pawlowski, Evil Superfarce, DJs Aldo & Dave

08
- 12 — Radio Centraal Bevrijdt de Muziek: Batto Lavoir Trio, Jozef van Wissum, Coin, Jean Michel Van Schouwburg, Kris Vanderstraeten, André Goudbeek Trio, E.A.S.L., José Bedeur & Jean Demey
- 23 — Psalters (US), Simple Brain & The Long Haired Ponchomen, The Owl Jolsons

09
- 13 — Festivaaalllaallal: Always Cry At Endings - Eisbär + Volxkeuken Deluxe
- 14 — Festivaaalllaallal: Always Cry At Endings - Eisbär, DJ Sickboy
- 15 — Ultra Eczema Festifaal: Frieder Butzmann (DE), Rudolf EB.ER's Runtzelstirn & Gurgelstock (JP/CH), Reijo Pami (FI), Sudden Infant (CH), Paul Labrecque & Mauro Pawlowski, Nuscht (DE/PL/BE), DJ Daniël, DJ Holland, Gora
- 20 — Festivaaalllaallal: Rococo Proefballon van Hotel Modern, Stef Lernous, Abbatoir Fermé, Steff's Super Sexxxy Spectacular Action Movies + Volxkeuken Deluxe
- 21 — Festivaaalllaallal Theater: Rococo Proefballon van Hotel Modern, Simon Allemeersch, Nicolas Delalieux, Giovanni Barcella, De Bokser en de Dood, DJ Croki + Volxkeuken Deluxe
- 22 — Festivaaalllaallal: A Cakehouse Present: 12 Piedestals (t.e.m. 29 september): Anton Cotteleer, Bart Van Dijck, Benjamin Verdonck, Dennis Tyfus, Guillaume Bijl, Guy Rombouts, Kati Heck, Lieven Segers, Lisa Jeannin, Michèle Matyn, Reinaart Vanhoe, Sven 't Jolle, Indianen Soapbox Racing Team, Godmode, Eisbär★ - Iglo: Me love my Global Warming, Heavy Indians, Maskesmachine, Boomhut door Benjamin Verdonck en Samuel, DJs Smalltown ss., Sorry Sexpartners, DJ Paniekzaaier
- 26 — Festivaaalllaallal: FC Bergman: 'De Rotsenbreker', Jellie Schippers, Sjoeke Maeije, Dahlia Pessemiers, Myriam van Gucht: 'Solveig'
- 27 — Festivaaalllaallal: FC Bergman: 'De Rotsenbreker', Jellie Schippers, Sjoeke Maeije, Dahlia Pessemiers, Myriam van Gucht: 'Solveig', J.X. Williams, Noel Lawrence: Other Cinema (US)
- 28 — Festivaaalllaallal: FC Bergman: 'De Rotsenbreker' Degurutini (JP) vs Mathieu Ha & Les Septembristes vs Kodomokyojin (JP), DJ Vidi Vici
- 29 — Festivaaalllaallal: P'tit Bataclan: CirQ, Slakkenman, Het Meisje met het Roze Jurkje Iglo: Me Love My Global Warming - Eisbär + Blotter Poet, De Kift (NL), Filip Kowlier, DJ Kid

10
- 05 — MuHKA_Media & Extra City Kinship Afterparty
- 06 — Heaven Hotel presents: Tiptoe Topic, I Love Sarah, Rabbit
- 12 — Van 't Straat Vannacht met Joesra en Evelien: The Dump Brothers, DJ Nohmada, DJ Naughty Nathan, La Fanfare Bizarre
- 14 — Ultra Eczema presents: Jad Fair (US), Lap, DJ Ghost, DJ Tyfus. Slides Alex Theuns, Film Carlos Aires
- 18 — Human Eye (US)
- 20 — Mokt meer lawijt! Perverz, A.M.O.K., DZL & Meta, Het Geluidssysteem, High Grade, 6Kill & Flix
- 21 — Think of One tryout (afgelast)
- *23* — Ultra Eczema presents: Wolf Eyes (US), Melted Men (US). ***Flyer by Dennis Tyfus & Kevin 'Apetown' Van Gaver***
- 27 — Mucom_Recordings present: DSR Lines, Forklong Daruplat, T.I.M., Ynri

2007

11
- 02 — Kakbek 2: Dreknek: Kid Kameleon, Miruki Tusko, Droon, Depotax, Kania Tieffer, Mr. Orange, DJ OOM.
- 07 — Kraak presents: Daniel Higgs (US), Grouper (US), Kiss the anus of a black cat
- 09 — Blackie & The Ohoos, Orphan Fairytale, DJ Inframan + Videoclip presentatie
- 16 — I H8 Camera, The Preludes, Datura
- 23 — Tulip, die Singende Tulpe (DE) + Volxkeuken
- 24 — De Macht van de Nuzikant! Battle of the Drummers: Alfredo vs Butsenzeller, Veni Vici DJ, de Gill pakt tram 3
- 28 — Envers-Swa presents: Papier Tigre (FR), Fordamage (FR), Gasoline DC, Kodiak, DJs Nachtschade, Makkaktraxxx, Fiktapeflex, Naughty Nathan
- 30 — Lost Film Fest (US) + Lab Waste (US)

12
- 01 — Balkan Beatz Antwerp Part 1: Antwerp Gypsy Ska Orchestra, Caspian Hat (NL), Hoppa Collective DJs
- 04 — Monotix (IL), Birds of Avalon (US)
- 07 — Kanaal.0 presents: Credi In Te Stesso, DCQ (NL), Röff (BE/NL), Charly en Gallus (NL), Tech-Matix (NL), Soi, DJ Uncle Fucker, DJ Libra, Visuals by Electric Sonatas
- 08 — Vague Angels (VS), Tanakh (IT), You Raskal You
- 14 — Lullabye Arkestra (CA), Stearica (IT), Boktor, DJ Visjus Rosko, Bruiling
- 15 — Poupi Whoopy 2: O's Devilles Harem Girls, Pussyshow Surprise Barbara Rom & Miss Incognito, Mummyshow with Creamy Caro, Mister Shiver and sexy assistant Lise, Balbaard, DJs Sorry Sexpartners
- 21 — Alaska Dawn, Lasergoat, WUV, Leafpeople, DJ Kid
- 22 — Ruffschool + jungle/dnb recordfair: DJ Trax (uk), Dago, Stekker, Havoc & Karbonkid, VJ Teknar

2008

01
- 07-08 — Workshop MAS in de Bache
- 21-25 — Workshop MAS in de Bache

02
- 01 — Openingsfeest 2008! DJ Croki, Alpha Male DJs + Volxkeuken Deluxe
- 08 — Sickboy and friends present 'Classick': Mr. Kill (FR), Monster X (UK), X&Trick, Sickboy & Droon + Volxkeuken
- *10* — Trumans Water (US), The Bugs (US), Oren Ambarchi (AU), DJ Mauro Pawlowski. ***Poster by Dennis Tyfus & Kevin 'Apetown' Van Gaver***
- 11 — Metroschifter (US), The Hickey Underworld, DJ with the Atom Brain
- *13* — Ultra Eczema Nachtlamp: Keith Rowe (UK), Sepie in Salsa Nera (cancelled), Tom Carter & Paul Labrecque (US). ***Flyer by Dennis Tyfus & Kevin 'Apetown' Van Gaver***
- 15 — Volxkeuken
- 16 — Hazavuzu (TR), Neat & Clean, Varkenshond, DJ Tyfus
- 22 — Seldon Hunt presents his ISIS documentary! + Volxkeuken
- 24 — Antistrot Party: Nisennenmondai (JP), Leprechaun Island (NL), Yobkiss + Syougo (NL/JP), Machinegewehr feat. Manny Blitzer (NL), Nothing Done (NL), Dr. Schnitt (NL), Dronkersbot (NL), Behringer Escape Plan (NL), DJs Boonie, Frenkelfrank, Remco, Beestkopf
- 28 — An Ultra Eczema Nightrider with: Eugene Chabourne (US), Eric Thielemans & Kris Vanderstraeten, Pumice (NZ), DJ Daniël, DJ J.A.C.
- 29 — Animus Anima, Bart Maris in Les Poubelles + Volxkeuken

03
- 07 — Infoavond Navo Game Over + Volxkeuken
- *08* — Radio Centraal Viert: 100 Jaar Internationale Vrouwendag. Brood en Rozen: Ida Dequeeker en Saida El Fekhri, Lore Van Welden, Silvia Erzeel + Karen Celis en Freya Piryns, Moniek Darge, Bea Cantillon, Anne-Mie Van Kerckhoven, Poppensnor, Miss Tigra, Lalupa, DJs Lampadair, Polly Vinyl. ***Flyer by unknown artist***
- *14* — Wewilllivestorm - Benjamin Verdonck + Kakbek 3: Music for Rabbits, Borokov Borokov, Miruki Tusko, DJs Mr. Orange, Dr. Drugz, Dustrickx. ***Flyer by Miruki Tusko & Robin Hectors***
- 15 — Envers-Swa presents: G.I.JOE (IT), Hypnoflash (IT)
- 20 — Film: J.X. Williams 'Other Cinema' - Noel Lawrence + The Celluloid Gurus (NL)
- 21 — Vette Party! DJs Visjus, Rosko & Bruinling, Missie + Volxkeuken
- 28 — Valina (AT), Codasync
- 31 — Envers-Swa presents: Sleeping People (VS), Bronze, De Pueda Matar, Gel for Michelle

04
- 04 — Volxkeuken
- 05 — 10 Jaar Ultra Eczema meer dan 1 jaar te laat: Grey Skull (US), Cassis Cornuta, DSR Lines, DJs Pelvis Slater And Headache, Patsbox Jean, Alphamale, JAC, Hanky Code, Brieno
- 10-12 — FC Bergman: 'De Rotsenbreker'
- 11 — Heartbreaktunes + Scheld'Apen presenteren: Pierced Arrows (US), To Live And Shave in L.A (US), De Bossen, Sudden Infant
- 12 — APEJOENG presenteert: Zion Lions, Das Estupando Orchestra, Thecray, Netsky
- 17-19 — FC Bergman: 'De Rotsenbreker'
- 18 — Cramarama: Nuslux (FI), Blaastaal, Amon Dude (FI), Kiiskinen (FI), De Kapkamer, DJ Pietcheval, DJ Ardelicious (FI), Jack De Rapper, Good Enough for You (AT), Der Tödlichen Trunkenheit Der Sinne

2008

04
- 19 Ruffskool 2: Pressure (IE/NL), Rhumble, Dago, Stekker, Karbonkid, Havoc + Record fair. ***Flyer by unknown artist***
- 25 Igor's Bubble Ball: Micro Capsule, W. Victor, Ambrassband, Angel Rodriguez, Lathem Dazès, Shady Dopperfield and Sinful Sindy, Benny Formaggio, The Sicilian Magician + Volxkeuken
- 26 Microob Halve Finale: Alaska Dawn, Ashrate, The Broadband, Power en de Mauz, Trio-Company, DJ Cauchy, DJ Komputerist, Mike_E
- 30 White Hills (US), Creature with the Atom Brain

05
- 02 Kuskessarma + Volxkeuken!!
- 03 Van't Straat Festival: Woesh, Los Gitanes, The Chicken Flyers, Tourist in Paradise, The Great Bulgarian Circus, The Name of Hector, Circo d'ell Fuego, L'amourgaga, Los Callejeros, La Fanfare Bizarre, Dunya
- 08 KDG PO expo: Present ourselves + Volxkeuken
- 09 Workshop Vegetarisch Koken + Volxkeuken Speciale + Infomoment E.V.A. + Film 'Our Daily Bread'
- 11 Apejoeng presenteert: 10 TON TET DJs Omegagirls, Alphamale Project, Townsound Smallsystem, DJ Fielip De Wienter
- 15 Pictures of Stares CD/LP release party: White Circle Crime Club, DJs Pisbroek Jean, Holland & Gohra, Bissy Bumsi, Live Feast Die Young
- 16 Mister Miyagi, Menschen Im Hotel, Buddiebunch (+ cliprelease by stout) + Volxkeuken
- 19 Heartbreaktunes and Kraak present: Pissed Jeans (US), Adolf Butler (NL), Vogue
- 23 Volxkeuken!!
- 24 Soirée Soleil: Crucial Alphonso, Wahwahsda, DJs Dreamtime Tjukurpa, Back 2 Bass, Roots Bamboo
- *30* 'Happy Day' - Ramsjgoed + Dozer Anniversary Bash 1998>2008: Raphaël, Stijn, Alexander, Murdock, Tinez + Volxkeuken. ***Flyer by Tom Tosseyn***
- 31 'Happy Day' - Ramsjgoed + Lavrendaff

06 ***Program Booklet by Afreux (Gino Bud Hoiting)***
- 01 'Happy Day' + Lavrendaff
- *06* Ultra Eczema Night: Justice Yeldham (AU), 16 Bitch Pile Up (US), Eekhoorn X, Bizzy Bunder (DE/A/BE/PL), DJs Faggot, Hank, Daniel, Pelvis Slater, Headache. ***Flyer by Dennis Tyfus & Kevin 'Apetown' Van Gaver***
- 13 Volxkeuken
- 16-19 Opvoering eindwerk laatste jaarsstudenten KCA
- 20 Volxkeuken
- *21* 10 Jaar Scheld'Apen!!! Rudy Trouvé Septet, Capsule feat. The Go_Tell (Elko Blijweert), Yobkiss (NL), Felix Kubin (DE), DJs Kid, Croki, Butsenzeller. ***Poster by Afreux (Tobias Debruyn)***
- 27 Apejoeng Presents: Dubstepjungleraggacore: Dubdelight, Bonafide, Dustrickx, Kifjar

07 ***Program Booklet by Janus 'Prutpuss' Lemaire***
- 04 The Love Company (ZA/BE), The Ray Pacino Ensemble (SE)
- 11 Apejoeng presents: Vandal X, Musth, Mount Venus + Volxkeuken
- *13* Radio Centraal's Quatorze Juillet: Pierre Elitair. ***Flyer by Kevin 'Apetown' Van Gaver & Dennis Tyfus***
- 14 Kraak presenteert Wooden Shjips (US), The Heads (UK)
- 18 Jazz! El Hafrado, Os Meus Shorts + Lunar 7
- 25 Jazz! Jeroen Van Herzeele/Giovanni Barcella Duo, Chaos of The Haunted Spire, Namid, Les Blauw; Club Rythmique de Belgique + Volxkeuken Deluxe
- 26 Elektrobel Summerfest Festival: In Cut Flower, Firefrog, Icteder, Disreality vs Elfenkommando, Bandarlog, Phollox, Harry Poppins, Cruizeoffiction

08
- 01 The Unholy Tree, The Joyous Cosmology` + Volxkeuken
- 08 Jazz! + Volxkeuken Deluxe: Eric Thielemans Feedbacking Fish, Backback
- 15 Heaven Hotel Festival: Damo Suzuki + I H8 Camera, Franco Saint de Bakker, Prima Donkey, Pox + Volxkeuken Deluxe
- 17 Theater Try-out Bizar
- 20 Made Out of Babies (US), Drums Are For Parades, DJ Crash & Burn
- 22 Apejoeng en Happy Twins presenteren: Maxnormal.tv (SA), Mount Zombie, IS-A DJ set, Makaktraxxx, DJ Paniekzaaier, No Star Crash, DJ 7anjers7rozen vs. DJ kinderarbeid
- *30* Radio Centraal bevrijdt de Muziek: Sheldon Siegel, Tricky CO., Eric Thielemans & Jozef Dumoulin, Collectief Reflexible, C. Albertijn-T. Campaert-T.Olbrechts, Prak. ***Poster by Dennis Tyfus & Kevin 'Apetown' Van Gaver***

09
- 12 Festivaaalllaallal: Benjamin Verdonck, Joke Van Leeuwen, Toon Tellegen, FTS Club Session 4 + Volxkeuken Deluxe
- 13 Festivaaalllaallal: Neat & Clean, Special Choir, Maskesmachine - De Weg, FTS Club Session 5 + De Klup, Kontra Kontainer
- *13-27* Festivaaalllaallal: Cakehouse Expo 'Het veld heeft ogen, het woud heeft oren': Joost Conijn, Heinrich Obst, Frank F. Casteleyns, Frans Van Praet, Goele de Bruyn, Lieven Segers, Maud Van de Veire, Michèle Matyn, Nadia Naveau, Nick Hullegie, Tina Schott, Ward Van Grimbergen. ***Poster by Nick Andrews***
- 14 Festivaaalllaallal: Kapitain Winokio - De Sprookjeskapitein, Gert Dupont/Froefroe - Billy The Tit, Special Choir, De Anale Fase, De Klup, Kontra Kontainer, FTS Club Session 6 + Volxlunch
- 15 Festivaaalllaallal: Eisbär - Collateral Damage, Nele Van Den Broeck + Kontra Kontainer, De Klup + Volxlunch
- 18 Festivaaalllaallal: Smartlapperij, Jules Krekel + Kontra Kontainer, De Klup
- 19 Festivaaalllaallal: Ramona Verkerk - Kamerdriehondervijftien, Simon Allemeersch en Nicolas Delalieux - There is a little café in Disneyland/Werk van tweeduizend en acht/2 + Tuning People - Worm + Kontra Kontainer, De Klup

2008

09
- 20 Festivaaalllaallal: Simon Allemeersch en Nicolas Delalieux - There is a little café in Disneyland/Werk van tweeduizend en acht/2 + Kontra Kontainer, De Klup
Ultra Eczema's Bruismelk festival: Coorz & Yeh (VS), Mommissar Hjuler & Mama bear (DE), Leslie Keffer (US), Raionbashi (DE), Pak (US), Sigtryggur Berg Sigmarsson (IS), George W Meyers (US), Pigs In The Ground (US), DJs Musketflickan, Tyfus, Daniel, Hank, Mond Vol Worst, Naughty Nathan, etc.
- 21 Festivaaalllaallal: Benjamin Verdonck & Willy Thomas - Global Anatomy + Kontra Kontainer, De Klup
- 24 Festivaaalllaallal: 8BITS Electronica Labo, Kontra Kontainer, De Klup
- 25 Festivaaalllaallal: 8BITS Electronica Labo + Gijs Gieskens (NL), Frau Holle (DE), 8GB (AR)
- 26 Festivaaalllaallal: Lisa Jeannin (SE), De Figuranten - Antigone, Geen Seute, Kontra Kontainer, De Klup, DJ Ghost
- 27 Festivaaalllaallal: Menno & Michiel Vandevelde en Jozef Wauters - Opera/Een werkstuk + Kontra Kontainer, De Klup + Bulbul (AT), Three Second Kiss (IT), Qui (US)

10 *Poster by Afreux (Tobias Debruyn)*
- 03 Volxkeuken
- 04 Dianogah (US), Bronze
- 10 Volxkeuken
- 17 Don Caballero (US), Kazuamsumaki
- 24 Ruffskool 3: Trax, Dago, Stekker, Karbonkid, Havoc, Visuals by Teknar & Blub Video
- 25 Scheld'Apen & Envers-Swa present: 31 Knots (US), Mutiny on the Bounty (LU)
- 27-28 Arbeid.Oderentweder. (try-out)
- 31 Volxkeuken

11
- 03 Lightning Bolt (US), Daniel Higgs (US)
- 07 Butsenzeller 'NATT' LP Release: Butsenzeller, Lars Lenders, Dieter Sermeus, Wingra, The Chocolate Lovers, Simon Lenski, Andrew Claes, The Lesbian Mouseclicks (NL)
- 14 Apejoeng presenteert: Codasync Cd Release! Codasync, Two Thirds of a Circus + Volxkeuken
- 21 Sickboy & Friends Turbo Jumper (UK), Dev/Null (US), Reverse Tunes (BR), D-agised, Igneon System, Mr.Orange
- 22 I.s.m. Heartbreaktunes: An Albatross (US), Yip Yip (US)
- 28 The Crappy Mini Band, Usutokine (JP) + Pieter Van Den Bosch - Toonmoment 2 + Volkskeuken Deluxe

12
- 05 Pieter Van Den Bosch - Eindpresentatie + Volxkeuken
- 06 Ruffskool 4: Raphaël, Havoc, Karbonkid, Stekker, Blub Video

2009

01
- 30 Kraak und Ultra Eczema terug vriend?!! U.S. Girls (US), Titmachine (NL), Hash Buffalo, DJ Tyfusschh
- 31 Kraak und Ultra Eczema terug vriend?!! Pain Jerk (JP), Emeralds (US), Birds of Delay (UK), Kraak DJs

02
- 06 I Love Sarah, Horacio Pollard (UK), Zwem (B/NL)
- 13 Sarah Benefiet + Volxkeuken Deluxe: Alex Agnew, Xander De Rycke
- *14* Poupi Whoopy 3: Harem Devilles in a Barbara Rom show, Dieven Act by Murielle en Jen, Creamy Caro, DJs Naughty Nathan, Victorine d'O, Sorry Sexpartners, Jungle Ferox with Creamy Caro, Rick Shiver and the savages, Eliz & Alice.
Flyer by Janus 'Prutpuss' Lemaire
- 19 I.s.m. Heartbreaktunes: Wolves in The Throne Room, Anaphylactic Shock (NL)
- 20 Volxkeuken
- 27 T&T presenteren: Deadsets, The Unholy Tree, DJ Frutsen Prutzer + Volxkeuken
- 28 Ultros Eczemos La Bamba Night(mare) LP presentatie + live: Remörk, Mauro Pawlowski, Benjamin Verdonck, Mitt Land Och Leo, Guy Rombouts, Babilon, Heavy Indians, Sheldon Siegel, Blaastaal, Glück und spass, Dolphins Into the Future, Ludo Mich, Dialogist Kantor Patacyclist, Autistik Youth, Emilio Lopez Menchero, Loops by Briener Schnitzel

03
- 06 Rijmtechniekers, Phillibustas, Nasta en Niz + Volxkeuken
- 13 Caro's Birthday Party
- *14* Kakbek 4: Return Of The Kak: Teddiedrum, Kania Tieffer, Miruki Tusko, Tex Taiwan, Musketflickan, DJ Nature aka DJ Raak Me Aan.
Flyer by Miruki Tusko
- 18 Tuning People Speelt Worm + Echo Beatty
- 19 Tuning People Speelt Worm + Tuning jam
- 20 Tuning People Speelt Worm + Old skool, jungle, rave + ... + Volxkeuken Deluxe
Tobscene - Marlies Vanhoucke + Ruffskool V: Stekker, Havoc, Karbonkid, Trax (UK), Nookie (UK)
- 27 Microob: The Flying Horseman, Nick Fransen, Tex Taiwan, Plastiks + Volxkeuken Deluxe
- 28 12 Jaar Ultra Eczema: Unicorn Hard-on (US), Wout Vercammen, Fyoelk (DE), Heini Obst, God Willing (US), Charles Berlitz (US), DJ Daniël, Lieven Segers

2
0
0
9

04
- 03   Ode aan JMH Berckmans: Billen, Sun Ra's Biblical Novotrip feat. Michiel Cox + Volxkeuken
- 04   Compagnie Frieda 'Kippen leggen toch eieren' + Enversswa: Aucan (IT), Pneu (FR), Shield Your Eyes (UK)
- 10   De Anale Fase + Volxkeuken
- 17   Matthieu Ha et Les Avrilistes + Volxkeuken
- 18   Mokt Lawijt III: Uberdope, Antraks, Shokproof, DJs Beatgrinders, Boom Syndicat, 6Kill
- 24   Apejoeng presents: DJupstoep: Mac 6/Jasper, Tapeshifta, Kastor & Dice, Goldorak & Solpher, Clinic
- 29   SLA-DAG: Silver River Swing Orchestra, Sopha, Lasvas Radio, Lama, Braindead Girlfriend, Sistaflex, DJs Nature, Dobbelterror, Tisse, Kid Camion, Alpha Males, Musketflickan, Jett

05
- 01   DLN & RUFUS 'Non Space' 7inch Release: DLN & RUFUS, Gasoline Stew and The Dump, Juliette et ses Baguettes, DJs Ungawa, lexa, Golbert
- 06   Expo/Mobile Unit: Afstudeerrichting Vrije Kunsten Sint Lucas Antwerpen
- 07-16   Braakland - Lotte Van den Bergh
- 08   Volxkeuken Deluxe
- 15   COITUS: Lucid, Chronic Sin, Igor, The Vains, Leave, with Vj Lennert + Volxkeuken Deluxe
- *16*   Ultra Exema's Coconut Beach Fest: Tomutonttu (FN), Ducktails (US), Lazy Magnet (US), Tamina Kiasinjan, DJs Pierre Elitair, Musketflickan, video's by Floris Vanhoof. ***Flyer by Dennis Tyfus & Kevin 'Apetown' Van Gaver***
- 19   Zwellend Fruit - PiusX Instituut (Try-out/premiere): Afstudeerproject Woordkunst-Drama
- 22   Apejoeng presenteert: Bodybuilding: NT89, G-Tronic, Nightrash, Tisse, Benni Moore + Volxkeuken
- 29   Elko Blijweert draait door! + Volxkeuken Deluxe
- 30   Van't Straat Festival: The Grezat Bulgarian Circus, El Circo d'ell Fuego, Dynamo Zjosss, The Cheap Clowns, Cafe Con Leché, Badabim Badaboem, Ambrassband, DJ Beatbutcher, DJ Dunya, DJ Dream Time Tjapurka

06
- 05   Volxkeuken Deluxe: DJ Inity
- 06   Apejoeng presents: The Quest for The Brown Note - Workshops, BBQ, Maximal Beats: Bandarlog, Ramses, Sanaki, Tension, Panda Pill
- 12   Volxkeuken Deluxe: DJ Visjus
- 13   Soirée Soleil: Polylinguals, The Subtitles, Sista Flex, DJs Turntable Dubbers, Roots Bambu, Saimn-I + BBQ
- 19   Afstudeerprojecten Theaterkostuumontwerp 09 + Volxkeuken Deluxe
- 21   Audities 'Only Ghosts Left To Play', Ragna Aurich
- 26   Geen Volxkeuken!

07
- 03   Film Klimaatactie + Volxkeuken Deluxe (Schuine Zomer)
- 10   Köhn, Dolphins into The Future, Jozefaleksanderpedro, DJs Hardrock Café (Ferraro) & DJ Charles Berlitz (Jack-o Motherfucker cancelled!)
- 17   Scheld'Apen & Heartbreaktunes present: Master Musicians Of Bukkake (US), Ignatz
- 24   11,000000001 Jaar Volxkeuken! Superdeluxe met dessert!
- *25*   11 Jaar Scheld'Apen!!! DJs Basketflickan, Borstpas, DJ Dheedene & DJ Drogba, Pfoeffbal.
  Flyers & Poster by Kevin 'Apetown' Van Gaver
- 31   School is cool! + Volxkeuken Deluxe

08
- *01*   Jaart Sail (Rommel-)markt: Stella, Afreux, Ward Zwart, Apetown, Yannick Val Gesto, Kraak, Funeral Folk, Conspiracy Records, Crama & meer. ***Flyer by Kevin 'Apetown' Van Gaver***
- 05-07   'De Grotenprins' - PG Robosto: Christoffel Hendrickx, Boris Uytterhaegen, Rob Kanters, Liesje De Smedt, Mark Suyckerbuik, Leen Scholiers, Filip Decoster, Astrid Bossuyt, Cazzimir Meulemans, Maaike Boot, Charlotte Deroover, Sam Vandenhoeck, Emilie Vloeberghs, Céline Mathieu, Nele Ooms, Rob Geersten, Ruben Boeren, Jonathan Lambrechts, Irina Schmitz
- 06   Volxkeuken Deluxe
- 13-15   Stage Lab presenteert: Kampvuur
- 14   Jazz! Les Blauw, Bear Guts Quintet + Volxkeuken Deluxe
- 20-22   Stage Lab presenteert: Kampvuur
- 21   Jazz! Dans Dans, Neruda, Eric Thielemans & Rudy Trouvé + Volxkeuken Deluxe
- 25   Ultra Eczema presents: Chris Corsano & Mick Flower Duo (US), Monopoly Child Star Searchers
- 26   Orgamusa, Vetex, Oblomov, S.W.A.N, Waterdans
- 28   Jazz!Feest!_Mushi Mushi_, Zoem Zoem, DJs Elko, Butsenzeller
- 29   Kakbek 5: Gansta's Paradise: Curse Ov Dialect (AU), Raaskalbomfukkerz (NL), THX1983, Normanhoffman, DJs Hugo Freegow, Paniekzaaier, Makkaktraxxx, Kak in het straatbeeld.

09
- 04   Feist der schmetterlingen: Mr. Orange + more + Volxkeuken
- 11   Volxkeuken Deluxe
- 12   Hell Thru Trip i.s.m. Kraak: GR (FR), Bear Bones, Lay Low (VE/BE), Foklong Daruplat
- 18   Cakehouse presents: Cakehouse: F.L.U.T., Ping Pong Tactics, Roman Louis Alexander Hiele, DJs Baba Electronica & DJ Lonely, Rufuzz, Musketflickan, Half a Sorry Sexpartner, works by Gerard Herman, Nel Aerts, Gilles Baeyens, Sine Van Menxel & Joke Lenoard, Shana Teughels, Yannick Val Gesto, Fréderic Lizen & Joëlle Batens, Lieven Segers
- 22   Los Siquicos Litoralenos (AR), Lazy Magnet (US), DJ Pinchade (AR), DJ Saxixa
- 25   Volxkeuken Deluxe

2009

09
- **26** — Ultra Eczema's Bruismelk festival: Charlemagne Palestine (US), Anton Bruhn (CH), Peter Fengler (NL), Ria Pacquée, Cotopaxi (DE). ***Poster by Dennis Tyfus & Kevin 'Apetown' Van Gaver***
- 26-27 — Voor Spoken om te Spelen - Ragna Aurich

10 — ***Program Booklet by Afreux (Tobias Debruyn)***
- 02 — Follow The Sound: De Wereld Als Trommel - presentatie biografie, Hazentijd première, Han Bennink trio & Noel Akchoté (NL), The Ex + Han Bennink (NL) + film + Volxkeuken Deluxe
- 03 — Follow The Sound: Oorwerk Night - Struttin' Like An Ipod Shuffle Hosted by Eric Thielemans: Jorgen Cassier, Jean-Yves Evrard, Peter Jacquemyn, Rudy Trouvé, Jozef Dumoulin, Lucio Capece, Louise Landes Levi, Sigrid Tanghe, Tom De Witte, I H8 Camera
- 09 — Sean Noonan's Brewed By Noon: Aram Bajakian, Shanir Blumenkranz, Sheldon Siegel
- 16 — The Germans + Volxkeuken Deluxe
- 17 — RA-event
- 21 — Scheld'Apen organiseert een 2de Tekendag
- 23 — Volxkeuken
- 24 — I.s.m. Heartbreaktunes: Magik Markers (US), Gunslingers (FR), DJs Nauthy Nathan, Musketflickan
- 29-31 — 'The Hidden Tracks' - Peter Aers & Tijs Ceulemans
- 30 — Hitch, Haymarket Riot (US) + Volxkeuken Deluxe

11
- 01 — The Paper Chase (US), John Vanderslice (US), Nomad
- 04 — Ultra Exemassa Hysterie: Hair Police (US), Floris Vanhoof, DJs Tonnen Zaad, DJ Daniel
- 06 — Volxkeuken Deluxe
- 06-07 — 'The Hidden Tracks' - Peter Aers & Tijs Ceulemans
- 13 — Am House, True Champions Ride On Speed, Galore + Volxkeuken Deluxe
- 15 — Workshop Zeefdrukken door de meisjes van Stella!
- 20 — Bang Bang My Baby + Volxkeuken Deluxe
- 26-29 — Songs on the Mahabharata - Theater De Spiegel (Avant-Première)
- 27 — Volxkeuken Deluxe
- **29** — Ultra Eczema's volksbijeenkomst: Women in the Woods, Marc Rossignol, Lliure Briz, Andrea Cammarosano, D. Tyfus + meer. ***Flyer by Dennis Tyfus***

12 — ***Program Booklet by Scheld'Apen, Apejoeng & others***
- 03 — Songs on the Mahabharata - Theater De Spiegel
- 04 — Songs on the Mahabharata - Theater De Spiegel + Volxkeuken Deluxe
- 05 — VIES FEEST! Shit & Shine (cancelled), Roman Louis Alexander Hiele, DJ Cavia, Kak in het Straatbeeld/Die Hard 3, DJ Kantoor, Air Cav, DJ Bramok
- 10-11 — Songs on the Mahabharata - Theater De Spiegel
- 11 — Codasync 'In Galoré' CD-Release: Codasync, Het Jäzz Kwärtet + Volxkeuken Deluxe
- 12 — Tropisch Excuus (Release Party CD Compilatiezine): Goo Baysick, Louis Hiele, Kurperbush, Willy Warmoes' All Star Band, W. Ravenveer, Remörk, EekhoornX, DJs Mambo Jean, Kristian Kretin, My Land and Lion
- 13 — Workshop Zeefdrukken door de meisjes van Stella!
- 14 — Volxkeuken Deluxe
- 19 — Poupi Whoopy IV: PouDude Release/The Men's Issue: Creamy Caro, Jean Biche & La Chose, La Fille d'O Harem Devilles, Ruben, DJs Jill & Ulrike Magic Poupi Team, Naughty Nathan, Sorry Sex Partners

2010

02 — ***Program Booklets by Afreux (Gerard Leysen)***
- **04** — Kakbek 666 Kak to the Future: Cupp Cave, Vaillante Racer, Midnight Galaxy, DJs Hugo Freegow, Paniekzaaier, DJ Bramok. ***Flyer by Miruki Tusko & Robin Hectors. Poster by Kevin 'Apetown' Van Gaver***
- **05** — Girls & Beasts i.s.m. Kraak: Gay Beast (US), U.S. Girls (US), Bird Names, DJs Gypsy Flemming, Shoothecat. ***Poster by Kevin 'Apetown' Van Gaver***
- 12 — Feestelijke opening van Volxkeuken Deluxe + Film 'Enjoy Poverty' - Renzo Martens
- 13 — Apejoeng presents: Blacklabel: Xhaust, Ditherkid a.k.a Selsius, Jett, Welcome, Air Cav, Mr. Orange
- 19 — Sir Richard Bishop (US), Jozef Van Wissem (NL) + Volxkeuken Deluxe
- 26 — Antwerp Gypsy Ska Orchestra, DJs AG/DC + Volxkeuken Deluxe

03
- 05 — Believo! 7" Release: Believo!, Ping Pong Tactics, Rape Blossoms + Volxkeuken Deluxe
- 06 — Fumertumer Party & Expo Grimm, Midnight Galaxy, Bedrugs, Wahwahsda?, Lama, DJs Bramok, Mr. Jones
- 09 — Ronan Riou Expo opening + Ronan Riou (FR) + Milan W
- 10-11 — Ronan Riou Expo
- 12 — Kakbek & Hands Like Birds slaan handen ineen: Gum Takes Tooth (UK), 1982, Penguins Know Why, DJs The Michael & Ongewenste Dischokees
- **13** — Ultra Eczema's Popcorn Night(mare): Poppemia Popcorn, Myland & Lion, Nikè Moens, Circus Bulderdrang, White Circle Crime Club, Benjamin Verdonck, Lode Geens, Kevin Apetown, Casa Nera, Jommeke Geeraerts, De Letterleggers, Vom Grill, Filip Vervaet, Floris Vanhoof, Ida Madonna, W. Ravenveer, Buffalo Simon, Fia Cielen, Stroheim, Nel Aerts, Jessie Schiettekatte, His Masters Void, Hantrax, Posessed Factory, Christophe Piette. ***Flyer by Dennis Tyfus & Kevin 'Apetown' Van Gaver***

2010

03
- **14** — Workshop Zeefdrukken met Stella
- **16-18** — Expo - Laurence Scherz
- **19** — Volxkeuken Deluxe
- **20** — Zie!Duif Speelt Stockholm: Tina Ameel, Yannick Bochem, Leen De Graeve, Sarah Demoen, Kathleen Treier, Ine Van Baelen, Katrien Van Wassenhove, Leentje Vandenbussche
- **21** — Workshop Zeefdrukken met Stella
- **26** — 'Silence Fini' Muziektheater, Giovanni Barcella, Jeroen Van Herzeele, Simon Allemeersch, Jozef Wouters, Bart Capelle, Muziektheater Vanzilverpapier + bESIdES Ensemble
- **28** — Workshop Zeefdrukken met Stella

04
- **01** — Bal Masqué (Academie): The Sapiens, Mon-O-Phone, Naked With You, Koala, Yah Tararah, DJs Goldfox vs Hellektronik, Kiss My Party, Jantjesbrooddoos, Vilto and Assassimon
- **03** — 13 Years Ultra Eczema: Peter Fengler (NL), Pierre Elitair, Toxoplasmosis (US), Alex Dumitran (DE), Jacques Beloeil (FR/UK), DJ Raphaël, DJ Daniel
- **09** — Volxkeuken Internationaal
- **09-10** — Latzi Jones - Cuaradio (Try-out)
- **16** — Volxkeuken Deluxe
- **16-17** — Heaven Hotel presents 'Coping With Video' - Dolby Surround for the poor: Aarich Jespers, Bart Maris, Rudy Trouvé
- **24** — Kakbek VII: License to Kak: Cartilage Rec, Internet2 (ES), Norman Bambi (FR), Scarlatti Goes Electro (FR), DJs Arc de Triomph (TH), Paniekzaaier, DJ Bramok, Die Hard 3 Pac
- **29** — SLA-FEST: The Piles, The Valleyhawks, Vortigyn, Deadsets, The Green Michelles, Silver River Swing Orchestra, DJ Tommy, Die Hard 3, DJ Benny

05
- **06** — Trans Am (US), Lazer Crystal (US), Midnight Galaxy
- **07** — Volxkeuken Deluxe
- **08** — Eugene Chadbourne (US)
- **13** — Vernissage Pop Art in het NICC (samengesteld door: Kati Heck, Lieven Segers, Dennis Tyfus & Michèle Matyn), F.L.U.T, Miaux
- **14** — Detlev/Oban performance/film + Volxkeuken Deluxe
- **21** — Cartune Xprez performance/film + Volxkeuken Deluxe
- **22** — Van't Straat Festival: Ell Circo d'ell Fuego, The Dump Brothers, Capsule, DJ Commax, Naughty Nathan
- **28** — MPB2 presenteert een buitengewone Walking EXPOoo

06
- **03** — Pop Art in het NICC (muziek gecureerd door Dennis Tyfus): Eekhoorn X, Helicoptere Sanglante
- **04** — Inhuldiging Voetbalstadion Petrolium Zuid! + Volxkeuken en receptie met DJ + Giovanni Barcella, Jeroen Van Herzeele, Andrew Claes
- **04-06** — 'De Kale Zangeres' - TG De Eenzamen (Eugène Ionesco)
- **05** — Lucky Dragons (VS), Milan W., Musketflickan
- **11** — Laatste Volxkeuken Deluxe
- **26** — Pop Art in het NICC (muziek gecureerd door Dennis Tyfus): Af Ursin (BE/FI), Mitt Land Och Leo

07
- **10** — Werkkamp 010 Openingsfeest + Voedselcollectief De Beek ft. Benjamin Verdonck, Silence Fini + Iva Bittove - Vladimir Vaclavek Deu (CZ), DAAU, School is Cool Scheld'Apen keuken en -bar. ***Poster by Afreux (Bert Depuydt)***
- **11** — Werkkamp 010: Dag van de gluurder voor al dan niet bejaarde kinderen! Jonny And Sybil, The Curious Case of Benjamin Zuddhist, Silence Fini + Scheld'Apenkeuken en -bar
- **17** — Werkkamp 010: Verdacht Vriendelijk: De Broers Karamazov - De Figuranten + James Blackshaw (UK), Machinefabriek (NL), Blatnova (NL), Dottir Slonza, Balbaard, Annelies Monsere, Forklong Daruplat
- **18** — Werkkamp 010: Totale uitverkoop! Dag van de gluurder: AMOK, Over de Speelbaarheid van maïs- en graanvelden, Masker, Gecrasht, Fort M8, Bonny & Clyde, Jaart Sail!, Bissy Bunder 'Beyonda' (film) + Scheld'Apenkeuken en -bar
- **24** — Werkkamp 010: D-Day: The Wolf, Death & The Acorn (SCO/IS/JP/NL/DK/ID/AT), N!euwe Supersolden, Milan Warmoeskerken & Erik Heestermans, Gnod (UK), Ecstatic Sunshine (US) + Scheld'Apenkeuken en -bar
- **25** — Werkkamp 010: Kijkdrift! Feest van de gluurder: AMOK, Four Quartets #4, FERNSUCHT, Nr.9: C1, 101, Op zoek naar Milena, LOTR Cyclus, Bonny & Clyde, SUN RA (film) + Scheld'Apenkeuken en -bar
- **31** — Werkkamp 010 Slotfeest!: AMOK, Tussenruimtes, FERNSUCHT, Four Quartets #4, Op zoek naar Milena, You Raskal You, LOTR Cyclus, Action/Dzialanie, Bonnie & Clyde, Bissy Bunder, Intangible States, Toonmoment (Simon Allemeersch), Dubbele gorie, Een oefening in Sterven II, Nr.9: D1+ Scheld'Apenkeuken en -bar

08
- **28** — Ultra Eczema's Voorlopige beëindiging van de zomer: Herb Diamante (US), George Mulford (UK), Miaux, DJs Daniel, Musketflickan, Le Grand Christian

09
- **03** — Terug Volxkeuken!
- **05** — Bulbul (AT)
- **09-11** — FC Bergman speelt 'De Thuiskomst'
- **10** — Volxkeuken Deluxe
- **10-12** — 'Janken en Schieten' Ilay Den Boer
- **17** — Volxkeuken Deluxe
- **18** — Part Chimp (UK), Moon Unit (UK), Dracula Lewis (RO), DJs Fyoelk, Matchbox Youth

2010

09		
	30	The Pink Flamingo Fusion Project (Han Swolfs, Elko Blijweert, Jeroen Stevens, Andrew Claes)
10		
	05-09	Dorp, Het verhaal van een uitzicht - Annelies van Hullebusch
	08	Toonmoment Barbara en Stefanie Claes 'Maar de wolven die leven nog' + Volxkeuken Deluxe
	09	Toonmoment Nicolas Delalieux 'LOTR Cyclus' + 10 om te zien!
	15	I.s.m. Kraak: Greg Malcolm (NZ), Sheldon Siegel, Ignatz
	16	C. Spencer Yeh & Okkyung Lee (US), EL-G (FR), TG (FR), DJs Shitting Cats, Musketflickan, video by Fia Cielen
	20	Quintron & Miss Pussycat (UK), Possessed Factory
	22	Ted Milton's Blurt (UK) + Volxkeuken Deluxe
	23	Demons (US), Sick LLama (US), Ludo Mich
	25	Cave (US), Spookhuisje, Improper Conduct
	29	Kakbek + Nutsclub = Kakclub/Nutsbek: Dynoo, Cupp Cave, Midnight Galaxy, THX 1983, DJs Paniek, Die Hard 3. ***Flyer by Miruki Tusko & Robin Hectors***
11		
	05	Codasync 'Snasycod' CD-Release: Codaync, Roman Hiele
	12	Prince Rama (US), Sun Araw (VS)
	20	Homeswinger Workshop Performance: Action Beat (UK), Gasoline DC, House of John Player (UK), Gasoline DJs
	26	'De Titiana Aarons Experience' door Tom Struyf
12		
	03	True Champions Ride on Speed CD Release!: True Champions Ride on Speed, Balanced Exposure
	04	'Layla Raqsa' Eindfeest voor de winterslaap!: DJs Cameltoe, Chili Poum, Mfetu, Strupar + meer! Visuals by Yannick Val Gesto + Bart Van Dijck

2011

01		
	28	Smerige Opening! Gay Beast (US), Child Abuse (US), DJs Naughty Nathan, Die Hard 3
02		
	04	Volxkonzert 01: You Raskal You & Friends + Eerste volxkeuken Deluxe 2011. ***Flyer by Rienk Michielsen***
	11	Volxkonzert 02: The Plow that broke the plains (film met live soundtrack) + Volxkeuken Deluxe
	18	A Clean Kitchen is a Happy Kitchen Album Release: A Clean Kitchen is a Happy Kitchen, The Ten Believers of Unheimlitec, Clean Happy Soundsystem
	19	Creep Street Interstellar Clouds Of Dust Cosmic Force (NL), BS-1 (NL), Paniekzaaier, Stroheim, X-Ray, Funkmaster Frits, Uinixxx, Desq
	25	Volxkonzert 03: Love Carb & Co, Lions & Lambs + Volxkeuken Deluxe
	26	Mokt Lawijt IV: Straatwaarde, Shockproof, Eigen Makelij, Turbulent Flow Show, Nasty Nag, Paniekzaaier
	27	Workshop Zeefdrukken met Stella
03		***Program Booklet by Afreux (Gerard Leysen)***
	04	Space Mates, Phynt + Volxkeuken Deluxe
	05	A Blackhand Records Night + 7" release party: Cherry Choke, The Skywalkers, DLN&Rufus, Zaam, DJs Philip Golbert, Freek Yellowstock, Swingalingta2, Hank the DJ
	11	'Werkkamp 010' filmpresentatie door Maxim Hectors Tette Niveau Marmer + My Bun is Fried, Byond Hills, Die Hard Bitchpack, Tampax, Muug Streetcred, Mamas Bitches
	12	Be My Guest presenteert: Das Fettfest: Sweet Ronny Moustache & His Horses, Wieter aka Fatima, Huis Mortier, Thunderdan & Pistolpete, Ugly Vicky, Mila Superstar
	16	Poino (UK), Trio It
	18	Volxkeuken Deluxe
	19	14 Years Ultra Eczema (paard1): Sunburned Hand of The Man (US), Tomutonttu (FN), DJs Daniel, Musketflickan
	20	Workshop zeefdrukken! Katrien van Stella + Workshop Puredata! met Hans De Ley
	24	14 Years Ultra Eczema (paard2): Kawaguchi Masami's New Rock Syndicate (JP), Golden Cup (IT), DJs Hank the DJ, Matchbox Jean
	25	Volxkonzert: Nimai, Static Dreams, Leave + Volxkeuken Deluxe
	26	Kakbek 10.1: Cocobryce (NL), Title, DJ Paniekzaaier & Friends. ***Flyer by Miruki Tusko & Robin Hectors***
	31	'Lonesome no more': Tip Toe Topic & Joris Caluwaerts + Les Blauw
04		
	01	'Lonesome no more' Tip Toe Topic & Joris Caluwaerts + Volxkeuken Deluxe
	02	'Lonesome no more' Tip Toe Topic & Joris Caluwaerts
	06	No Age Plays 'The Bear': No Age, DJ Matchbox Youth (wccc)
	08	Dream or Die!: Stellar om Source, Kristy Foom/Modern Witch, W.Ravenveer, Louis Hiele, DJs Stroheim, D Jasfrikaans, DJ Nature, VJ Val Gesto + Volxkeuken
	15	T@ngo & Ca$h M. Hectors Film-Benefietfeest in 3D: DJs Die Hard 3 PAC, Mauro, T.Vanhamelen, Makatraxxx, My Bun is Fried, Pomrad, Fabriek, Ellentje Wils + guest: Molly Flappy
	20	Farhilda presenteert 'Welkom in mijn bed'
	22	Kapitan Korsakov, Deer, DJ Bukkake Fever + Volxkeuken Deluxe
	23	Kabek 10.2: Jealov, Pudding 00, Lopti, Mills Boogie, Die Hard 3, Bramok

2011

04
- 28 — You can't have your cake and eat it (in Academie): Bert Jacobs, Gerard Herman, Liesbet Grupping, Nel Aerts, Tom Poelmans
- 29 — Basketball (CA), Razen + Volxkeuken Deluxe

05
- 03 — Barn Owl (US), Jefre Cantu-Ledesma (US), DJ Warsaw
- 06 — Dream or Die 2!: Chris Corsano/Dennis Tyfus Duo, Milan W/Louis H, Mills Boogie, Sharrivarri, Bramok + Volxkeuken Deluxe
- 13-16 — Scheld'Apen op de Ankerrui: Sofie Van Der Linden, Frederik Heyman, Decap Muziekmakerij: Andrew Claes, Jon Birdsong, Jurgen Desmet, Dago Sondervan, Jürgen De Blonde, Youri Van Uffelen, Roman Hiele, Emiel Redant, David Van der Weken, Cakehouse Expo: Bert Huyghe, Florence Raats, Michiel Ceulers, Mil Ceulemans, Sofia Boubolis, Tom Poelmans, Stijn Bastianen, Koen Delaere, Xavier Noiret-Thomé
- 15 — Jaart Sail!
- 18 — You can't have your cake and eat it: De kunstenaar praat op woensdag: Liesbet Grupping
- 20 — B. Kael Feest: Carwash (KNBL), Kapsalon het paard, Kevin Poppe + Volxkeuken Deluxe: Wereldkeuken
- 21 — Zomes (VS), Kogumaza (UK)
- 25 — You can't have your cake and eat it: De kunstenaar praat op woensdag - Gerard Herman
- 27 — Volxkonzert: Sukilove
- 28 — Kakbek 10.3: Surf Kill Label Night: Dynooo, Cupp Cave, DJ Wesley C, Jar Moff, Ssaliva, Salted Slugs, Die Hard 3 Pac

06
- 03 — Volxkonzert: Herbert Eckardt (DE/IT/US) + Volxkeuken Deluxe
- 10 — Creep Street: Unicorn Hard-on, Container, Laser Poodle, Eekhoorn-x, Fyoelk, DJs Doobie Bros, Paniekzaaier, Stroheim, Azer + Volxkeuken Deluxe
- 16 — Abe Vigoda (US), DJs Naughty Nathan, Abe Vigoda DJs, The Michael & I like you guys already
- 17 — Volxkonzert: King Dalton + Volxkeuken Deluxe
- 24 — Laatste Volxkeuken Deluxe
- 28 — Zak Patat 2 BBQ Summer Edition: Franklin Barefoot, Winther, Jahfar, Mr. Garageband, Timberino master of the guitar hero, DJs Paniekzaaier, The Nutty Producer, Bonafide, Vincent & Manu, Gonzo, Thimberdome

07
- **01** — Start 'Werkkamp 011': Opening Vies Festival: Vies Feest: Farid Fabriek, Judo Club, Die Hard 3 Pac, Deadbeat vs The Deck live, Louiske, Kanta Vagana, DJ 7 anjers 7 rozen. **Poster by Jonas De Decker & Benny Van den Meulengracht-Vrancx**
- 06 — Trankiel Tornooi
- 07 — Dream or Die 3: {&apos + xtns}.play, Cuppcave, L Hiele, DJs Simonhild, Walrus, Millz Boogie, Visuals: Yannick Val Gesto
- 08 — Hakken over de sloot expo: Benny Van den Meulengracht-Vrancx
- 14 — Quatorze Juillet de Radio Centraal: Dutronic & Juliette et ses baguettes, Pierre Elitaire, Daniël Le Botaniste
- 16 — Werkkamp openingsfeest: Buvette (CH), Felixbrod-Harari-Ziblat (IL), Jozef van Wissem (NL/US), Hellvete, Miaux, Edgar Wappenhalter, Mittland och Leo, DJ Matchbox Youth + R Stevie Moore (US), Bed Rugs, I Love Sarah + Opening van De Vuilen Hond
- 17 — Werkkamp 011: Dag van de Gluurder: Sweet Isolation - Security Blotting, Triomff Triomff, Dries Beugels, Kinderenvandevilla - Don't stand so close to me - composition #1
  Werkkamp 011: Doorlopend: Emanation Labs (Sander Michiels en Renée Simons), Zoological Institute for Recently Extinct Species (Jozef Wouters en Menno Vandevelde), Kati Heck & Kasper De Vos, Jana Cordenier, Lore Schuerman, Zsofia Bene, The Great Nordic Sword Fights, Gitte Le Bruyn, Alexandra Maignan en Melanie De Groot van Emblem, Café De Vuilen Hond
- 19 — Workshop Zeefdrukken door Stella
- 22 — Pannekoekbeach: Pomrad, Pudding 00, Casual Harassment, Fabrik + Val Verde
- 23 — Werkkamp 011: D-Day: Alexander Tucker (UK), Cactus Truck (NL), Gum Takes Tooth (UK), BRLâAB, Flying Horseman, False Friend + Apejoeng vs Fornication Hi Fi
- 24 — Werkkamp 011: Dag van de Gluurder: Jaart Sail
- 26 — FEESTDAGDAGFEEST: Apejoeng Allstarz DJ Team, MASsief, DJ Nature, Val Verde, DJ Muug Street Cred, Sexy l'MC, CYNTHIA, Kanta Vagana + Workshop Zeefdrukken met Stella
- 28 — Drrraw Brrrawl: tekenavond
- 29 — Premiere Jabberwocky + Drrraw Brrrawl: expo + Vies Einde
- 30 — Werkkamp 011: Feest van de Gluurder! The Great Nordic Sword Fights, Swimmers in Loch Ness, Sara Clissen, Dead Dog 1999, Sanne Van Giel, Sander Michiels, Roel Swanenberg, Oshin Albrecht, Nike Moens & Vick Verachtert, Myriam van Gucht, Jellie Schippers & Douwe Dijkstra, LVMM, Lore Schuerman, Katrien Declercq & Laura Vandewynckel, Kasper De Vos & Kati Heck, Jozef Wouters, Jana Cordenier, Jan van den Bleeken, Vincent Van Dijck, Ine Bettens, Gentuza, Hanne Foblets, Gitte Lebruyn, Gautier Oushoorn, Dries Beugels, Daan Maltese, Charlotte Grandgaignage, Barbara & Stefanie Claes, Anna Innokentyeva, Alexandra Maignan & Melanie De Groot van Embden, Zsofia Bene

09 — **Program Booklet by Afreux (Gerard Leysen)**
- 02 — Feestelijke heropening van de Volkskeuken
- 03-04 — 'Collapsus' - Ragna Aurich & Kurt Vandendriesche
- 09 — Mac Bennie Burgerpaleis + Jasper TX (SE), Kaboom Karavan, Kosmische Keuterboeren
- 10 — Tweek Bird (US), Bad Body (UK), Tangled Horns
- 16 — Volxkeuken Deluxe
- 17 — 'In progress, a symphonic poem about life' - Gents Universitair Symfonisch Orkest, Andrew Claes, Bert Dockx, Vincent Brijs, Han Swolfs, Lynn Cassiers
- 23 — Electronic Music Films: The Delian Mode, What the future sounded like + Volxkeuken Deluxe

2011

09
- 29 — Cam Deas/Jack Allett Duo Score 'Decasia' + Film
- 29-30 — 'Roest' - Silke Melis, Simon Van Brandt, Anton Geerts

10
- 01 — Mill's Boogie-Night: Mills Boogie, Internal Sun, Die Maschinenanbeter, Collapsing Radio Force Mantras, Roman Hiele, Redrey a.k.a. Chicago aan de Schelde, Raphaël, Tinez, The Cubic Animal a.k.a. Brassmonkey
- 07 — Sheldon Siegels Hand in Eigen Boezem + Volxkeuken Deluxe
- 07-09 — 'Troost' - Leonard Muylle
- 14 — Sheldon Siegel en Radio Centraal: Gedeelde Smart: Cassis Cornuta, Musketflickan, Zoot Rufus, Hank The DJ
- 15 — Zak Patat: Boulet Edition: Franklin Barefoot, The Monotrol Kid, The Jokers, Timberino & Sugar Matson, DJs Die Hard 3 Pac, Bad Turntablism, Farid, Manu, Dubberdiedubdub Dubdub Dub, Superbock & Wally The Nut + Volxkeuken Deluxe
- **21** — The Beautiful Band, Sylvester Anfang II, Urpf Lanze, Floris Vanhoof, Bear Bones, Lay Low. **Poster by Bent Vande Sompele**
- 22 — 'Gecrasht' - Ahmed Khaled
- **24** — Ahleuchatistas (US), One Man Team Dance/Theo (UK), True Champions Ride on Speed. **Poster by Bent Vande Sompele**
- 28 — Sheldon Siegel Tast in het Duister + Volxkeuken Deluxe Sheldon Siegel, Koen de Roovere, Milan Warmoeskerken, DJ Matchbox Jean

11
- 04 — Combineharvester (CH), Vincent Van Dijck + Volxkeuken Deluxe
- 11 — Viesss Feest: Irani De Coninck, Die Hard 3 Pac, Mills Boogie, Kanta Vagana + Volxkeuken Deluxe
- 18 — Electronic Music Films: Deconstructing Dad, Bassline Baseline, DJ Roman Louis Hiele + Volxkeuken Deluxe
- 24 — Ultra Eczema moet blazen: An electronic dance pudding: Heatsick (UK), Design a Wave (UK), DJ Raphaël, DJ Daniel
- 25 — Volxkeuken Deluxe
- 25-26 — Fleischmann - Leen Bogaerts, Amara Reta, Maartje van Bourgognie, Nico Boon
- **26** — Gangpol und Mit (FR), Eekhoorn-X, DJs Bramok, Val Verde, Dragon. **Flyers by Miruki Tusko**

12
- 02 — Codasync Akronize Album Release + Laatste Volxkeuken van 2011
- 03 — Eindfeest voor de Winterslaap: Layla Raqsa 2, DJs Bramok & Hiele, CaMEL TO€, Jugoton, L€Blanc, $TrupAR

2012

02
- 03 — TV Centraal Startshow: Radio Centraal
- 10 — The Final Pomp: Vogue, Citizen's Patrol (NL), Reproach, Black Haven, Your Highness, Toxic Shock, DJs Tok en Danny + Volkskeuken
- 11 — Enversswa Presenteert: Jef der Dood Trio, Khuda, Birdbrain, The Deer Friends, Star Club West, A Horse called Turkey, DJs Die Hard 3 Pac, Mills Boogie, Farid Fabriek, My Bun is Fried, Gorgeous Underworld
- 16 — Cabaret Dr Strange: Herb Diamante, Primordial Undermind, Bridget Hayden, Head of Wantastiquet + more
- 17 — Robbie Basho 'Twilight Peaks' LP presentatie: Glenn Jones (US), Je suis le petit Chevalier (FR/BE), Tristan Driessens
- 24 — Dream or Die 4: Craxxxmurf, Mills Boogie, Rotary Cuff Repair, Louis H, DJs Tinez and Raphaël, visuals by Yannick Val Gesto en Christian Oldham
- 25 — Ultra Eczema Partij: Body/Head (US), Kim Peers, Musketflickan, DJ Daniel

03
- 01 — Sailors beware
- 01-03 — 'Halve Mens' - Tuning people
- 02 — Wannes Deneer
- 09 — Electronic Music Films: Practical Electronica, Chromasonics, EMS 8 + Volkskeuken Deluxe
- 10 — Ooh Wee: Ballin': DJ Skype, Beatbutcher, Team Panini, Mills Boogie, Val Verde, Die Hard 3 Pac, DJ Natte Dröm, Fabriek
- 16 — Champagne Champagne (US), Good Idea, Darrell Cole (UK), Nasty Nag, Die Hard 3 Pac + Volkskeuken
- 17 — Sing Star Holocaust: Vampire Blues (UK), Banana Head (US), Matthew P Hopkins (AU), Benjamin Franklin, DJ Cool Brocoli, DJ Lieven Moana
- **21** — Ultra Eczema's Lenteviering: Thurston Moore Noise Gig, W. Ravenveer, DJ Geraldine Hermans, DJ Jane Mathyn. **Flyer by Jef Cuypers & Dennis Tyfus**
- 23 — Volkskeuken
- 23-24 — 'De Optimisten' - Hanne Foblets, Hanne Struyf, Louis Van der Waal
- 31 — Bletchly Rules! Fest: Action Beat, Don Zero, Hired Muscle, Duke of Zuke, Bad Body, The Sense of Adventure Tape Deck Orchestra

04
- 06 — Hare Akedod II: Razen + Suchet Malhotra (IN), Steffen Basho-Junghans (DE), Niels Voaals, Regression (US), H&H Slaughter (US), DJs Bent Von Bent & Für Dich Verlag
- 07 — Neptune (US), Jason Van Gulick (FR), Kamperen in Frankrijk
- 14 — Zak Patat: Partysnacks Editie: Toolbox live, Vince the Prince, Paniekzaaier, Project, Dr Brambo & DJ Arab, Tymus, G Smooth
- 14-15 — 'Alfre(d)o' - Sara Vilardo, Nele Vereecken + 'Collapsus' - Ragna Aurich, Kurt Vandendriesen
- 19 — SLA-FEST: Hertje, Claustrophobic and the Escalators, Interesting Television Programs, DJs Die Hard 3 Pac, Fabriek, Mills Boogie
- 10-21 — 'Maart 2012 (Wanneer paarden sterven)' - Theatercollectief Tibaldus
- 20 — Blue Ridge Mountain Fest: Black Twig Pickers (US), Yann Gourdon & Yvan Etienne (FR), Family Underground (DK) + Kraak DJs
- 26 — Feest van de Architectuur: The Hidden Creators, The Renegade Orchestra, Tessy Ray's Bell, DJ Reynders, Santana Soundsystem
- 27 — New Music For Old Instruments: Cian Nugent (IR), Stephan Mathieu (DE), Jozef Van Wissem (NL), Sir Richard Bishop (US), Urpf Lanze, Gonzalez & Steenkiste (VE/BE) + Volxkeuken

2012

04
- 29 — Common Festival: Joyous Cosmology, Matt Watts and the Calicos, Inneke 23 & Miss Rectangle, The boy that ate his glasses, U-boat, ONI, Equinox, the peacekeeper, Antwerp Deadheadz, Don K Posto and his 3 chord band, Jaymanplan, Nimai and the songbuddies, Red Case, Lady Angelina, Less Mansardez, Glenn Wouters, Bert Gabriels, Nigel Williams, Vincent Van Meenen en Jan Dertalen, René Broens en Mieke de Loof, Babenko Belgium, Antistresspoweet, Amanda Malinka, Alois De Beuseleir, Didi de Paris, Frans Vlinderman, Christoffel Hendrickx, Marc Schepers, DJs Doortje, King Flashman, DJ Simon, DJ Lemakuhlar B2B Smooth, DJ Swing'a'thing, DJ Moonchild, Sam Kbam de echte, Electric Lord, One Sixty, Chopstick, Harry Bordelle, Ozman Project

05
- 04 — Electronic Music Films: 'Totally Wired' + Volxkeuken + Andreas Schneider workshop
- 05 — 2000 'n High presents: Jack Playmobil Releasenight, Rude 66 (NL), Hungry Soul, Redray, DJs Raphaël, Stellar om Source, Ruby Rage, Gonzo
- 05-06 — 'Het Fantastische Leven van de Heilige Sint-Christoffel zoals samengevat in twaalf taferelen en drie liederen' - Simon Allemeersch, Barbara Claes, Stefanie Claes, Silence Fini
- 11 — Layla Raqsa III: Awesome Tapes from Africa, Basketball, DJs Cameltoe, Strupar, Maj Tahal, Cinnamoon, Bramok, Sharivari & Hiele
- 12 — FC Trankiel Foaf 2: Sexy l'MC, Cordon, K-Tight, Gin en Juice
- 18 — De Bomma's Toonmoment: Nike Moens, Vick Verachtert + Volxkeuken + Bvba Delalieux (work in progress)
- 25 — Om ter Luidst - Maxim Hectors: Nier Van A, Fabriek, Kinderarbeid, DJ 7 anjers 7 rozen
- 31 — 15 Jaar Ultra Eczema Deel 1: Ghedalia Tazartes-Chris Corsano-Dennis Tyfus trio (FR/US/BE), Diamond Catalog (US), Daniel, Musketflickan

06 *Program Booklet by Afreux (Bert Depuydt)*
- 01 — Volxkeuken Deluxe
- 07-09 — 'Land's end' - Berlin
- 15 — Sunn 0))) (US), Aluk Todolo (FR) (in Fort 8)
- 26 — Zak Patat: Dogs of Cibola, Mantaray, Toolbox, Nickson Beatbox, DJs Vince the Prince, Stronk, Trust the kid, Kobe Louis Charles, Project Bonzai, K-Tight, Dail A Mamas

07
- 06 — Feestdagdagfeest: Jo Serrano, DJ Filip, DJ Chingchangchong, DJ Loesje, Dr Dog, DJ Ananas, Sexy l'MC, Windows 3000 & Vaneeshua, Puss Puss
- 08 — Jaart Sail + Brunchlunchmunch (zolang de voorhuid strekt)
- 13 — Wei Feest: Tinejoris, Anderthaler, Jangle Boist, Ephiciel, DJ Loe + Zomers Volxkeuken Deluxe
- 14 — Quatorze Juillet de Radio Centraal: Pierre Elitair, Daniel le Botaniste, Les Hommes U
- 15 — Zondag Smosdag + Brunchlunchmunch (zolang de voorhuid strekt)
- 20 — Las Kellies (AR), Beach + Volxkeuken Deluxe
- 21 — Ooh Wee: Ballin' II: Internal Sun, Mixmonster Menno, muteBoy, DJs Natte Dröm, Val Verder
- 22 — De Groene Gorgel + Voetbal Frenzy
- 25 — Workshop Zeefdrukken met Stella
- 27 — Pertang Deel 1: The Dwarf Empire - Sanne De Wilde, DJ Lady E en Lisa Tuf, Archimedes, DJ Raak me aan vs DJ Kinder@rbeid, Lermotov + Zomerse Volxkeuken Deluxe
- 28 — Pertang Deel 2: The Dwarf Empire - Sanne De Wilde, hoola hoop workshop - Filles de Minuit, Lien Anniceart, Hannah De Meyer, Greet Jacobs, Vincent Van Meenen en Jan Dertaelen, Hertogs Haast - van Muur Mûr(e) project, Eva De Baets en Peter Hendrikx, bvba Delalieux, Roestbox, Shenandoah special
- 29 — De Tuin van eten

08
- 03 — Bild und Sturm: DJ Funni, Musketflickan, Faesbinder, Judo Club + Zomerse Volxkeuken Deluxe
- 05 — Fris & monter + Workshop Zeefdrukken met Stella
- 10 — Unicorn Hard-on (US), Container (US), Laser Poodle (NL), Moemlien, Marcel Du Swamp, DJ Lieven Moana, DJ Snoid, DJ Foom + Zomerse Volxkeuken Deluxe
- 11 — Reiziger, Syndrome
- 12 — Iedereen Verdoemd + Brunchlunchmunch (zolang de voorhuid strekt)
- 15 — Workshop Zeefdrukken met Stella
- 16 — Otark at Scheld'Apen
- 17 — Zomerse Volxkeuken Deluxe
- 17-18 — 'You may find yourself' - Sofie Palmers & Katrien Pierlet
- 19 — Caoutchou's Lazy Sunday: Drafter (DE), Ninjato, Spongemagnet, DJs Stubborn & Leftchest
- 24 — Stupid Bright Confetti, Crippled Nerdface, DJ Natte Dröm, DJ Raak me aan vs DJ Kinder@rbeid, DJ groetjes Jozef & DJ hallo met Jonas + Zomerse Volxkeuken Deluxe
- 26 — De laatste zullen de eerste zijn + Jaart Sail + Brunchlunchmunch (zolang de voorhuid strekt)

09
- 06 — Flestivalalal 2012: Openingsgladiatorenstadionrockfest: David Bovee, In-Kata, Younes Faltakh, Tine Van den Wyngaert, Charlotte Vandermeersch, Kim Peers, Philip Fierens, Judo Club, Simon Allemeersch, Jozef Wouters, Kasper De Vos, Nicolas Delalieux, Afreux, Kati Heck, Tina Schott, LVMM, Sigo Bram, Mattias Cré, Jorg Strecker, Gerrit Muylaert, Hendrik Muylaert, Kris Delacourt, Sander Cruz, Pieter Van den Bosch. *Flyer by Afreux (Tobias Debruyn)*
- 07 — Flestivalalal 2012: De Conferentie Deel I: Benjamin Verdonck, Bernard Van Eeghem, Frans Zwartjes (NL), Daphne Verhelst & Emma Lesuis + De Conferentie Deel II: Peter Fengler (NL), Tiago Sousa (PT), Pieter Van den Bosch, Takashi Ito (JP), The Unholy (SE/NL)

2012

- 09
  - 14 — Flestivalalal 2012: Benjamin Verdonck + John Birdsong + Jutta Troch + Otark Filmdiner
  - 15 — Flestivalalal 2012: Ultra Eczema's Bruismelk Festival en 15 jaar Ultra Eczema deel 2: Sven-Ake Johansson (SE), Coolhaven (NL), Eli Keszler (US), Ashley Paul (UK), Mss Meesterd 6, Ninos Du Brasil (IT), DJ Ali Meurs, DJ Faesbinder
  - 16 — Flestivalalal 2012: Coping with video Rudy Trouvé + Lonesome no more: Tip Toe Topic & Joris Caluwaerts
  - 19 — Hare Akedod III: Expo 70 (US), Ancient Ocean (US), Sunny Dunes (FR), DJ Bent Von Bent, DJ Lieven Moana
  - 20 — Flestivalalal 2012: De neus - Nike Moens + De bultenklacht - Barbara & Stefanie Claes + Tien Stenen - Nicolas Delalieux
  - 22 — Flestivalalal 2012 Eindfeest: Razor Blades - Paul Sharits (US), Sheldon Siegel lp presentatie, Somadamantina (ES), Lee Patterson (UK), Floris Vanhoof, Janek Turkowski (PL), Varkenshond (NL/BE), Stacks, Suicide on Hawaii (FR/BE), Je suis le petit Chevalier (FR), Indianan's Evil Eye, Huur is Duur
  - 23 — Flestivalalal 2012 De Epiloog: Appelpersfestijn, De Fietskeuken, Paul De Graaf, Peter de Batist, Jacques Tempère
- 10
  - 05 — Volxkeuken Deluxe
  - 06 — Toxic Shock, Dry Heaves, Filler, Cheap Drugs, Kids Insane
  - 11 — Jooklo Duo (IT), Gonzales & Steenkiste
  - 12 — Fungus + Kamperen in Frankrijk + Volxkeuken Deluxe
  - 18 — Volxkeuken Deluxe
  - 18-19 — De Bomma's - Feikes Huis, Compagnie Frieda
  - 20 — Scorpion Violente (FR), The Dreams (FR), Twilight Racing
  - 23 — Cliffor Torus (NO/UK), Staer (NO)
  - 26 — Ooh Wee Ballin': Vuurwerk a.k.a. Jealov, Nasty Nag, Natte Dröm, Fabriek, Val Verde, Mills Boogie + Volxkeuken Deluxe
  - 29 — Zeefdruk workshopweek (t.e.m. 2 november): Jelle Kindt
- 11
  - 02-03 — 'Wereld, einde van een' - Compagnie Frieda
  - 03 — Doomsday Students (US) (in LLS 387)
  - 09 — She Sells Seashells, Soldier's Heart, Hear Hear a Cheer, DJs Clint Easthood, Bukakke Fever + Volxkeuken Deluxe
  - 10 — Charanjit Singh (IN), Heems (US), DJs Stellar om Source, Stroheim, Redray, Jan Techniks
  - 16 — Zak Patat: Toolbox, Mask, Vince the Prince, Flapjack & Arno Lemmens, Flying Carpets, Ralph Collier, Project, J&J
  - 17 — Up High Collective, Moodprint, DJ Natte Dröm
  - 22 — Hare Akedod 5: High Wolf (FR), Plankton Wat (US), DJ Bent Von Bent
  - 23 — Kontra 16mm Filmvertooning: 'Slow Action' - Ben Rivers + Otark Volkskeuken
  - 28 — Thulebasen (DK), Fyoelk (DE)
  - 30 — Common Café: René Broens & Mieke de Loof, Didi de Paris, De Auteur, Equinox The Peacekeeper, Michael Lamiroy, Eigen Makelij, Symmethree, DJ Chopstick, DJ Swing'a'thing
- 12
  - 07 — 0090/Off Instanbul: Klaustro (TU), Kim Ki O (TU), Proudpilot (TU)
  - 14 — Kontra 16mm Filmvertooning: 'Heiligabend auf St. Pauli' - Klaus Wildenhahn + Eenzame Kerstnachtfeest: DJ Für Dich Verlag + Kerstvolkskeuken

2013

- 02
  - 02 — Nachtwinkelfeest: Beach, Ping Pong Tactics, DJs Irani De Coninck, Vanessa Omega, 3j
  - **09** — **Zak Patat: Loempia Editie: DJ Raak me aan, Enzo, Bear Thrill$, K-Tight, Project, Sexy l'MC, Juicy & Jazzy, Wally.**
    Flyer by Benny Van den Meulengracht-Vrancx
  - 10 — Scheld'Apen in de beek: Repaircafé met Tile Vos en Kris Delacourt (in De Beek)
  - 13 — Mykki Blanco (US), Born Gold (CA), Tinez, Fabrik
  - 14 — Urpf Lanze LP release, Sayona, Remörk, Hare Akedod (in Audioplant)
  - 15 — Wereldkeuken: Rwanda
  - 21 — Otarkino: 'Life in Denmark' (in Klappei)
  - 22 — Make a Scene: Blackbird, North, St. Francis
  - 23 — Jack Playmobil presents: Fastgraph (NL), Hantrax, DJs Pametex, Stellar om Source, Raphaël, Stroheim, Hungry Soul + Nachtwinkel: Open Shop
- 03
  - 01 — TV Centraal 2.0
  - 09 — Nachtwinkel: Performance Ruud Ruttens/Eva Vermeiren + Ooh Wee: Toolbox, DJ Esch, OohWee DJs, Yardie Bass
  - 10 — 'Een stroper, zijn dochters en een harpij' - Maxim Hectors (in Klappei)
  - 14 — Rhyton (US), Mik Quantius + Dagora (DE/NL), DJs Füngels & Sloow (in Audioplant)
  - 15 — Wereldkeuken: Afghanistan
  - 16 — Bild und Sturm II: Batia Suter, Ruud Ruttens, Vaast Colson, Gerard Herman, Luke Norman, Nik Adams, Dominque Somers, Ward Heirwegh, Lot Doms, Benjamin Demeyere, Brecht Vandenbroecke, Wafa Baccaert & Wouter van Riessen, DJs AA & Shoot the Cat, Geen casanova's! cha cha cha, DJ Fatigué, DJ Surprise
  - 18 — Druk druk druk expo - Jelle Kindt
  - 23 — After Six Festival: Black Coffee, The Phantoms, The Stubs, Vvhile, Dead Neandertals, Moaning Cities, ATH1281, Marie Err, Essay Dee, Stefan Unkovic, Nick Alston, Ricardo Cavolo, Kruella d'Enfer, AkaCorleone, David Penela, Luke Pelletier, Bcn Sea, Jangojim, DZIA

2
0
1
3

03
- 24   After Six Festival: Scarlett O'Hannah, Little Boy, Slowcoaches, Témé Tan, Charles Howl, Savanna
- 29   Otarkino 'Divine Horsemen' (in Pekfabrik)
- 30-31   Workshop Zeefdrukken

04
- 05-07   Scheld'Apen presents: Duivels groeten met gesloten oog - Bent Vande Sompele (in Hole Of The Fox): Ark Tablet + Hare Akedod 005: Tape Presentatie
- 08   Springtime Ceremony: A story of rats, Bird People, Vallona, Gonzalez & Steenkiste
- 12   Wereldkeuken: Congo
- 13   Palmboomfeest: Pêchen in Blik, Soldier's Heart, Die Wunderkinder, DJ Thuglife, Daniel de Botanicus
- 13-14   Workshop Zeefdrukken
- 18-20   'Persona 2013' Tibaldus en andere hoeren
- 21   Welvaert Welton - Time Circus (in Bonapartedok)
- *26*   Ooh Wee: Lisbent (DK), DJ Paypal (US), Twilight Racing, R. Hiele, OohWee DJs. ***Flyer by Tomas Opinao***
- 27   Openfortacht: Tom Volkaert, Lennart Van Uffelen, Romeo Van Snick, Ministry of Mass, Jelle Kindt, Ozge Akarsu, Nicolas Delalieux
- 30   Deaf People Audio presents: No Joke Seriak, Snez Beast, Freddy Bracker, Poldoore

05   ***Program Booklet by Afreux (Bert Depuydt)***
- 02   Children of the White Leaf, Yannick Franck, Le Supralitoral of Brown Noise + No Flag
- **04-05**   Scheld'Apen op de Beurs: Maakba(a)r, Saskia Van der Gucht & Vader Cosemans, Voedselcollectief de Beek, Kasper De Vos, Solarshop, De Nachtwinkel, Bild Und Sturm, Bries, Extrapool/Halfwithal, Harmonie, Fabrikage, Truus Keustermans, Tapesale Distro, Ultra Eczema's Mss Meesterd, Fur Dich Verlag, Sheldon Siegel's Greve Totale, Studio Fluit, Mayken Craenen/Huis Haas, Barbara Vandecauteren, Wannes Verhees, Renée Simons, John Birdsong, Izja Rutten, Quiet Days Records, Ministry of Mass, Narelle Dore & Sigrid Volders, Johanna Trudzinski, Thomas & Hannes Deville, Jelle Kindt, Apetown, Topokopie.
  Flyers by Afreux (Gerard Leysen)
- 08   Innercity feat. Sloow, Ignatz, DJs Sapi & Cheworee Safari
- 11   Nachtwinkel: Gerard Herman, Olivier Smets + Common Art Café: Geert Lenssens, Babenko Belgium, Waldrada Onzea, Isabelle Vanasche, Sarawut Chutiwongpeti, Bendt Eyckermans, DAAD, Encq De Ruddere, Audrey Lauro, Grossadmiraal Dimi, Mos Graffiti, Reversed Graffiti, Fanfare Fatal, Franklin Barfoot, Gentlemen Unexpected, ONI, Alois de Beuseleir, Zilla & Alphonse, Educated Foolery, Globe Trotter, Higgs B2B Guerney Champion, Kolonel Woezli, Lito & Chung, MVMNT, MINT, Omni Mill, Tempest, Amanda Malinka, Antistresspoeweet, Audrey Lauro, Vincent Van Meerbeeck, Yannick Moyson, Katakuma, La Belle Vert
- 15   Szilard plays 'New sound works for the short films of T. Nishikawa' + Skybox + Volkskeuken
- 18   Gum takes Tooth (UK), Author & Punisher (US), DJ Sickboy
- 23   Otarkino op locatie: 'Werner Herzog eats his shoe' - Les Blank
- 25   De Nachtwinkel: Hypnos Book Launch - Jozefien Gruyaert
  Fabrikage: Jah Heavy Load, Mixmonster Menno, Bobby James Family, Ifa Y Xango, BRZZVLL, Kingstux, Spongemagnet, Uphigh Collective, Leftchest, Herr Pies, El Neoray, Jangojim, Marie-Charlot Vleminckx, Charlotte Dumortier, Timothy De Rycke, Luca Kortekaas, Kevin Welslau, Bramok, Cazzimir, Julianne Noll, Dzia, Vagabundos, Gun-T, Ligone, Topo, Linksone, Bisser
- *31*   Ekster Label Night: Hiele LP release: Hiele, TCF (NO), RP GM KRC (Ssaliva & Dynooo), DJs Tomislav, Techniks, Mills Boogie. 'Kamelen en Muzieken, een concert door de bourgeoisie' - Barbara en Stefanie Claes en Siso Marco Polo.
  Flyer by Victor Robyn. Poster by Barbara & Stefanie Claes + Siso Marco Polo

06
- 01   De Nachtwinkel: Floris Vanhoof
- 07   Syria, seriously?: Eric Todts, Annabell Van den Berghe, Akram Hano, Pieter Stockmans, Die Hard 3 Pac, Mills Boogie, Oui Les Filles
- 08   Phantom Radio: Gerard Herman, Julie Peeters, Nicolas Matranga, Matthew Kneebone, Soft Temple II, Ward Heirwegh, Mittland och Leo, Ine Meganck & Valentijn Goethals
- 13   Chuck Johnson (US) (in Audioplant)
- 14   Wereldkeuken: Joost
- 14-16   Waanzin: An Onghena, Freya Clijmans, Julie Van den Meutter, Linde Luyten, Linde Brockx, Tille Lingier + Baf Bonjour
- 15   De Nachtwinkel: Music for Nightshops 7" release: Milan W., Molnbâr av John (SE) + Workshop Zeefdrukken
- 16   Open Noord: Scheld'Apens mobiele zeefdrukstudio
- 20   Usssy (RU)
- 21   De Nachtwinkel: Midsummernightshop: Corbyn Mahieu, Of the holy blood, Kia Tasbihgou, Andreu Serra, Ultrazapping, Sebastian Zimmerhackl, Timon Mattelaer, Jules Peter, Tim Colmant
- 22   Workshop Zeefdrukken

07
- *06*   15 Jaar Scheld'Apen: Volksdansfeest: Daniel de Botanicus, DJ JK Rowling, Jah Mathe, Mills Boogie, Bramok, Fabriek, Bent Von Bent, Leliboi123, DJ Raak me aan vs DJ Kinder@rbeid. ***Flyer by Afreux (Gerard Leysen)***
- *12*   Jooklo und Metabolismus (IT/DE), Congregation of Spirit (CL), Colavittel (BE/DE/CL). ***Poster by Bart Sloow***
- 13   Zak Patat: Vegi Burger edition
- 19   Otarkino 'Daisies'
- 20   Feestdagdagfeest: Bobby Conn (US), Apejoeng DJs, Honey Duuzend, Bent Von Bent & Bram Roest met u, Kak in het Straatbeeld, Mills Boogie, Sexy l'MC, Apejoeng goes Epic
- *26*   Ultra Eczema's Annual Bruismelk Festival: Matt Krefting (US), Monopoly Child Star Searchers (US), The After Lucy Experiment, Sharon Gal (UK), Astor (UK). ***Flyer & Poster by Dennis Tyfus & Gerard Herman***
- 27   Rodeofest 2013: Colaris (DE), Monomyth (NL), Bliksem, Aguardente, San Diablo, Your Highness, The Reeves, The Guru Guru, We'rewolves, Toxic Shock, My name is God, This Kid, Produkt

2013

08
- 02 — Ignatz en de stervende honden, Indias Indios, Orphan Fairytale + Wereldkeuken: Korea
- 03 — Jaart Sail + THX + Cupp Cave, Hiele, Laserpoodle (NL), Hauser/Quaid, Paniekzaaier
- 09 — Jon Birdsong Latenight Situation09-10
- 09-10 — Mandy Niewohner + Skybox Zomerkeuken
- **09-24** — Bookers & hookers #1 'De Verdwijning' - Nico Boon, Hanne De Backer, Ine Bettens, Aurelie Di Marino. **Flyer by Gerard Herman**
- 10 — Grovgast
- 16-17 — Jovial Grégoire Mbenga & Nele Vereecken + Skybox Zomerkeuken
- 17 — Congregacion de Espiritus: Live opnamesessie
- 22 — 'De vrijetijdsmens' - L'Hommmm + Skybox Zomerkeuken
- 22-23 — 'Daniil' - Nicolas Delalieux, Roman Hiele
- 24 — Deviant Release - Benny Van den Meulengracht-Vrancx & Yannick Val Gesto: DJ Raak me aan, DJ Bebilove, DJ Leliboi123, DJ Sizzler_007, DJ Bent & Bram
- 25 — Otark's Garlic & Jazz: Joachim Badenhorst
- 28-29 — Keuperskaai + Skybox Zomerkeuken 'De Schepping/The Creation'
- 30 — Barbara Claes - Akaaremoertoe Bahikoeroe/Lezing van een toneelstuk - Myriam Visschoonmaker, Stefanie Claes, Philippe Flachet, Nicolas Delalieux, Nico Boon, Jan Bijvoet, Simon Allemeersch, Hendrik Hein Van Doorn, Nathalie Goossens + Ahmed Khaled: toonmoment Wereldkeuken: Nepal
- 31 — Dag Zomerdag: Jelle Kindt, Johannes Rodenacker (DE), Tomoko Mori (JP), GRISFX, Ward Zwart, Bent Vande Sompele

09
- *08* — Destination Earth: Hieroglyphic Being (US), Inner City, Hungry Soul, DJs Zoot Ruff Ski, Cosmo Knex, Hantrax, Raphaël, Hiele. **Flyer by Johann Kauth & Rufus Michielsen**
- 15 — DJ Hvad
- 20 — Fritzi und Heidel (CD release), Ratzinger, Jean DL, DJ Han
- *21* — Date Palms, Plankton Wat, A Dance to Music From the Guard House - Siet Raeymaekers & Lieven Moana, DJ Bent Von Bent & Reverendo Treintaitres. **Flyer by Bent Vande Sompele**
- 24 — Ultra Eczema's Dwanghekken: Black Pus (US), èlg (FR), DJ Allon Kaye (UK), DJ Re Do. **Poster by Dennis Tyfus & Jef Cuypers**
- 27 — Carate Urio Orchestra (album release), Sean Carpio Solo + Wereldkeuken: Tibet
- 28 — Op Rollertjes Rollerdisco: Musketflickan, Zoot Ruff Ski & Cosmo Knex

10
- *12* — Inhuldiging
Het Laatste Eindfeest!!! Robedoor (US), Team Panini, Sickboy, Nieuwzwart Trio, De Heer Tyfus, Sand Circles, Dynasty, Floris Vanhoof, Daniel De Botanicus, Mills Boogie, Orphan Fairytale, Gerard Herman en ontzachelijk veel meer. **Poster by Afreux (Gerard Leysen), Polyprint**

varia

Volxkeuken/Volunteering/Cooperation/General information

varia 01: Flyer by unknown artist

varia 02: Poster by unknown artist

varia 03: Note by unknown artist

varia 04: Flyer by unknown artist

varia 05: Flyer by Iwan Verhulst

varia 06: Flyer by Jelle Crama

varia 07: Flyer by Bent Vande Sompele

varia 08: Flyer by Janus 'Prutpuss' Lemaire

varia 09: Flyer by unknown artist

varia 10: Note by unknown artist

varia 11: Flyer by unknown artist

varia 12: First graphic work by Dennis Tyfus

Epilogue
BentenBenny

It has been an instructive two year journey of collecting works, archiving and going through the process of making this book. We have enjoyed that journey immensely, scouring through the rich imagery and reinvigorating old friendships along the way.

Additionally, we worked long and hard on a "complete" agenda of Scheld'Apen from beginning to end, with over 1300 events, which we decided to incorporate in the book. We hope you enjoy finding the events you may have attended, remeniscing a legendary night.

We would like to thank all the artists who have ever created a flyer, poster or program booklet for Scheld'Apen. Your work is truly unique. Without you, we would not have been able to make this book.

We would like to thank all collectors, you who have kept these works safe for 10 years or more. Without you also, we would not have been able to make this book.

We would like to thank Het Bos, Tile Vos and David Van der Weken for your enthusiasm and hospitality.

We would like to thank the Royal Academy of Fine Arts Antwerp and Nico Dockx, of research group ArchiVolt, for their guidance and support during the archival process and for hosting the book launch and accompanying exhibition.

We would like to thank Stockmans Art Books and Bruno Devos for believing in our project and the realization of this book.

We would like to thank Pieter Willems, Roel Griffioen and Pia Jacques for your textual contributions, and Matthias Meersmans for translating Roel's text.

We would like to offer special thanks to Freya De Quint and Eline Willemarck.

Furthermore we would like to thank Elko Blijweert, Radio Centraal, Joachim Cols, Karen Cosemans, Jelle Crama, Wannes Cré, Els De bruyn, Sofie Dederen, Lotte De Voeght, Jasper Der Kinderen, Yannick Val Gesto, Robin Hectors, Roos Janssens, Johann Kauth, Janus 'Prutpuss' Lemaire, Gerard Leysen, Lieven Martens, Kurt Marx, Jan Matthé, Sis Matthé, Michèle Matyn, Rufus Michielsen, Fred Nasen, Daphné Pascual, Vettig Patje, Mia Prce, Daniël Renders, Vincent Royers, Joery Scheepers, Lieven Segers, Dieter Sermeus, Sjoerd Stolk & OCCII, Eric Stroheim, Tom Tosseyn, Dennis Tyfus, Saar Van de Leest, Eva Van Deuren, Kevin 'Apetown' Van Gaveren, Annelies Van Opstal, Raphaël Vandeputte, Dave Vanderplas, Benjamin Verdonck, Peter Verwimp, Martijn Vogelaers, We Are Various, and last but certainly not least: Gilles!

'Graphic Design of Scheld'Apen' is the result of two years of collecting works, three archival residencies at Het Bos and a short scanning residency at Frans Masereel Centrum.

The project is a collaboration between artist
Benny Van den Meulengracht-Vrancx and
musician Bent Vande Sompele, Het Bos and
The Royal Academy of Fine Arts Antwerp,
under the guidance of Nico Dockx.
All work by Benny and Bent was done voluntarily.

This book was made possible with the support of
The Royal Academy of Fine Arts Antwerp, AP Hogeschool,
Stockmans Art Books and Het Bos.

Art direction, planning, editing:
Benny Van den Meulengracht-Vrancx and Bent Vande Sompele

Design:
Benny Van den Meulengracht-Vrancx and Bent Vande Sompele

Cover design:
Benny Van den Meulengracht-Vrancx and Bent Vande Sompele

Text:
Pieter Willems, Roel Griffioen and Pia Jacques

English translation of 'Een Grafische Bodemstaal' by Roel Griffioen:
Matthias Meersmans

Photography:
David Van der Weken (toilets) and Steven Decroos (posters)

Scans:
Benny Van den Meulengracht-Vrancx, Bent Vande Sompele
and Jan Matthé

Contributing editors:
Bruno Devos, Nico Dockx and Wouter Van der Wangen

Publishing:
Stockmans Art Books

Coordination at publisher:
Bruno Devos

Production:
Royal Academy of Fine Arts Antwerp and Stockmans Art Books

Print:
1200 books were printed in Duffel, Belgium.
First edition ©2023
ISBN 9789464363395

Artwork crediting:
The publisher and makers of the book have tried to reach out to each and every creator or owner of an artwork and have credited them correctly. Any creator or owner of an artwork that is currently uncredited, please contact the publisher.

All rights reserved. No part of this publication may be reproduced, distributed, stored in a retrieval system, or transmitted in any form or by any means, graphic, electronic or mechanical, including photocopying and recording, or otherwise, without prior permission in writing from the publisher, except in the case of brief quotations embodied in critical reviews and certain non-commercial uses permitted by copyright law.